REDSTONE'S
Guernsey & Jersey Guide,

OR THE

STRANGER'S COMPANION

FOR THE

ISLANDS OF GUERNSEY AND JERSEY:

CONTAINING

A BRIEF DESCRIPTION OF THE PUBLIC BUILDINGS, ANTIQUITIES, AND SCENERY,

WITH

AN ACCOUNT OF THEIR LAWS, PRIVILEGES, CUSTOMS, TRADE, AND BIOGRAPHICAL NOTICES.

TO WHICH HAVE BEEN ADDED, IN THIS EDITION,

THE LEGENDS, SUPERSTITIONS, AND CUSTOMS OF GUERNSEY;

ALSO SOME SPECIMENS OF

THE GUERNSEY PATOIS.

BY

Louisa Lane Clarke,

Author of " Recollections of Sark," " The Country Parson's Wife," &c., &c.

SECOND EDITION.

GUERNSEY:
HENRY REDSTONE, ARCADE LIBRARY.
LONDON:
SIMPKIN AND MARSHALL.

———

1843.

PREFACE

TO THE SECOND EDITION.

THE first edition of this little Guide was very hastily compiled, to meet an urgent demand; this second Edition has been carefully corrected, and much enlarged by a collection of the Superstitions of the Island, and some specimens of Guernsey Patois; also, by adding to the usual notices of public Buildings and public Places such more unknown Walks and Legends as may give new interest to our beautiful Island.

But, as from the nature and size of the volume, the History and Laws of Guernsey have necessarily been briefly mentioned, the Stranger is referred to Mr. Redstone's Library, where from "Jacob's Annals of Guernsey," every information may be obtained.

A sketch of the sister island Jersey has been written as a companion to the Guernsey Guide, and bound up with it, for the convenience of those who visit both islands. Jersey is *very* beautiful, the inland scenery differs from, and is superior to, Guernsey—and much of its pe-

culiar attraction lies in the hitherto unpublished
beauty of its secluded valleys and ancient winding ways, to which this Guide will often refer.
A limited time and space have compelled me to
be very concise in all my directions; I feel
that injustice is done to both these lovely spots
by any mere outline, therefore must advise the
Traveller to refer to Inglis's Channel Islands for
a better acquaintance with Jersey.

Louisa Lane Clarke.

June, 1843.

TABLE OF CONTENTS.

JERSEY.

in Guernsey

THE

GUERNSEY GUIDE.

——————

CHAPTER I.

THE stranger who visits these islands (and well are they worth a visit, as the annual influx of wanderers from all parts of the world most surely proves) will doubtless make some inquiry as to its discovery and early settlement; and though the present intention of this little book is not to enter upon any learned disquisitions on the antiquities of Guernsey, or give any elaborate history of its laws and government, yet, in pointing out the objects best worthy of attention, it will relate whatever may invest them with additional interest.

Guernsey is situated in the Gulf of Avranches, within sight of the French coast, 49° 28' N. lat., 2° 40' W. lon., about 120 miles from Southampton, 75 miles from Weymouth, 60 from St. Malo, 28 from Jersey, and 21 miles from Alderney between which places a constant and almost daily communication is kept up by steamers through out the year.

B

The shape of this island is triangular, or rather resembling a harp, elevated towards the south, where the coast is broken into the most picturesque bays, runs out into bold rocky headlands, and falls precipitously to the sea; then shelves off towards the north, where the fine sandy beach is rendered almost inaccessible by a complete chain of rocks thrown like a girdle round the coast.

The circumference is about thirty miles, its extreme length about nine and a half, and its extreme breadth about five and a half.

Guernsey was formerly called the Holy Island —"La bien-heureuse Ile Sainte." It was thus named by the monks who came to the island in the year 996; but, even antecedent to the Christian era, it was celebrated for its sanctity, and dedicated to Saturn, or Gwyn, or, as Cæsar gives it, to Dis Pater—Dieu le Père. Besides which, legendary lore attributes its freedom from all venomous animals and insects to the particular blessing of St. Patrick. By all geographers it is called in Latin "Sarnia;" (*Vide Jacob's Annals of Guernsey*); sometimes, also, "Granoria," or Isle of Rocks.

Guernsey was well known to the Romans, who have left their footsteps behind them in several ruined fortifications on the island; but little is ascertained of its early history, until it was bestowed upon Sampson, Bishop of Dol, in Brittany, by Childebert, son of the first christian king in France. In the year 1035, Robert, Duke of Normandy, caused the channel islands to be annexed to the bishopric of Coûtance, under whose jurisdiction they remained until Queen Elizabeth annexed them to the see of Winchester. Since the time of William the Conqueror they have always been under the British Crown, but enjoying the privilege of their own Norman laws and government.

On approaching this island, the Casket Rocks will probably have arrested the attention. They are enormous rocks, upon which lighthouses were erected in 1723, after a petition from the Gover-. nor of Alderney, Peter Le Mesurier, Esq., in consequence of the immense destruction of life and property from the fearful state of the Channel at this point. For about a mile in circumference these rocks lie scattered in one great cluster, the water round them varying from no less than twenty-five to thirty fathoms. The great rock upon which the lighthouses are built is thirty fathoms above the level of the sea; three towers, placed in a triangular position, connected by walls, which form an area in which a few vegetables are cultivated by the keepers, who are persons from Alderney, supplied with necessaries from the island, and receiving a salary of fifty pounds per annum from government: they have no fresh-water spring on the rock, though some time ago a very small but pure stream was discovered by the pigeons kept there. It has dried up, however, and they depend upon rain-water and supplies from Alderney, with which they communicate by means of a small telegraph, or by lighting a fire on the rock.

After passing the Caskets, the approach to

Guernsey is very beautiful; the rising ground to
the south is studded with trees, churches, wind-
mills, villages, and gentlemen's seats. The old
Vale Castle, and Mont Crevet battery, with the
harbour of St. Sampson between them, and on
the other side a group of picturesque islands—
Serk, Herm, and Jedthou—the town of St.
Peter's Port, rising from the sea to the summit
of a very high hill, flanked on the right by Fort
George, and fronted by the ancient Castle Cornet,
form an amphitheatre of no ordinary beauty.

Some years ago, St. Peter's Port was designated
as a " little market town, consisting of *one* long
narrow street, which has a good magazine, and is
thronged with merchants." (See Dicey's Guernsey). When it was first built does not appear decided, but probably all the rest of the island was
more or less peopled; for we find amongst the
ancient churches, that of the town was the *tenth*
and *last*, consecrated on the 1st of August, 1312,
at which time two chapels were in use dedicated
to St. Julien and St. Jacques. The town may
be divided into the old and new, though of the
former little really remains, except a few old
houses near the town church, Horn-street, and
Tower-hill.

The barrières include all the lower part of the
town, Fountain-street, Mill-street, Smith-street,
and the Pollet. These are entirely devoted to
shops and mercantile offices, store-houses, and
water-mills; they are narrow and gloomy, presenting but a discouraging view at the first approach. New Town, together with Hauteville,

have altogether a different appearance; they are built with great order and regularity, containing some fine buildings, excellent dwelling-houses, and as many delightful residences as can be met with near any town in Europe.

The number of inhabitants at the last census, (1831), amounted to 24,349.

CASTLE CORNET

Being the first object of attention on arrival, we shall give a slight account of this ancient fortress, which stands upon a rock of gneiss, everywhere crossed and intersected by veins of quartz, of trap, and of felspar, placed about six or seven hundred paces from the shore; so that at high tide it is a complete island, whilst at low water a safe passage on foot may be effected over its rocky bed. The tradition of a Roman origin for this castle is devoid of foundation, for it appears that it was erected by Raoul de Valmont, a governor sent to Guernsey by Henry II., when contesting the crown with Stephen. (*Mr. Le Marchant's MS., quoted by Jeremie, p.* 123). During the parliamentary wars, Sir Peter Osborn, Lieutenant-Governor, attached to the king, held the castle for a long period against the rebels, and kept three Commissioners of the Parliament, Messrs. Des Granges, De Havilland, and Peter Carey, prisoners, from which confinement they escaped at low tide in a most extraordinary manner. In 1672 this castle was struck by lightning, when

Lord Viscount Hatton was governor, who was miraculously saved, though his wife and mother, the Dowager Countess Hatton, were killed, with the servants. His two sisters were preserved by the falling of a beam, so as to prop the roof of their room, and his two infant children were found uninjured; one of them in the arms of a dead nurse, the other in its cradle. The lightning had struck the magazine, which thus destroyed a great part of the old buildings. When fully armed the Castle mounts upwards of fifty pieces of ordnance, and has both artillery and infantry barracks, store-houses, a spring of good water, furnaces for red-hot shot connected with almost every battery, and bomb-proof apartments for 300 men.

It is necessary for strangers to obtain a pass from Government House in order to visit it; and from the upper battery and flag-staff there is a beautiful view of the whole eastern coast of Guernsey, with the line of cliffs to the south, as far as the promontory of Jerbourg, on which a column is seen called Doyle's Pillar.

———

THE HARBOUR

Was first ordered to be built by Edward I., A. D. 1275; who directed that a duty of twelve sous tournois should be levied on all ships, and six sous tournois on all boats arriving in the island. However, from some misapplication of these sums, and delays from time to time, nothing was done till the year 1580, when the work was commenced at the South Pier, and continued without intermission until it was completed. It is about 250 yards in length, the North Pier about 150; they are both about 35 feet in height, and protected by parapets. Though strongly built and capable of containing about 100 sail, small crafts and vessels of considerable burthen, ships of 700 tons and even frigates, having put in during stress of weather, yet its size is so inadequate to the great increase of commercial enterprise, that various plans are now under consideration for the building of a new Pier, which will be of the greatest advantage to the island in every respect, and another monument of the patriotism and indefatigable spirit of our much-respected Chief Magistrate, the present Bailiff of Guernsey. At the western extremity of the South Pier is the Guardhouse, where, during war time, a guard of thirty men were stationed under the command of a commissioned officer; but a sergeant's guard of four men is now more than sufficient for the assistance of the police, whose strong room joins the building, and whose services are but very seldom required in this orderly and peaceful island.

THE TOWN OF ST. PETER'S PORT.

Hotels and Lodging-houses.

The principal hotels are in High-street. Marshall's hotel is situated in an open part of that street called the Carrefour, the general lounge for all idlers, and meeting-point for men of business, having the Post-office* on one side, the Club-room on the other, and Smith-street, leading from it to the upper part of the town, and into the country.

Gardner's hotel is lower down; and at Shore's boarding-house, and Dadson's boarding-house, a cheap and comfortable residence may be obtained for any length of time. Furnished lodgings may be obtained in any part of the upper town from fifteen shillings to two guineas a week: of these, the best are, Mrs. Claypole's, Ridout's, Grumley's, Chant's, and Collings'.

Supposing, therefore, that the stranger is comfortably settled in one of these, we shall briefly sketch the principal buildings which may be worth visiting in this parish.

The Parochial Church.

The parochial church, of Gothic architecture, is built entirely of granite; and the porch on the north side is worthy of observation, with its pointed arch and deep archivalt mouldings of granite; as are also the massive pillars in the interior, which support the tower and the arched roofs of the aisles, formed of blocks of dressed granite. The walls are embellished with a number of monuments and cenotaphs, several of which are tasteful and elegant. In 1821, when the church underwent a thorough repair, in laying open the

* Post-office removed to the Commercial Arcade. Postmaster, Captain Fell; Assistant-Postmaster, Le Mesurier.

North-East chapel an ancient niche was discovered, which appears to have been formed at two
different periods, the upper stones being of the
same granite as the portico of the north entrance,
and carved on the same model; the two imposts,
with the lettuce leaf in high relief, are of Caen
volite, and appear of more modern workmanship:
three or four other niches were discovered at the
same time; and also an octagonal baptismal font
of shell marble, with its pillar, was found buried
under the steps leading to the Ecclesiastical
Court.

The beautiful embroidered Genoa crimson velvet which ornaments the communion table and
pulpit, was originally brought to the island from
France by the mother of the present Earl of
Shaftesbury, for a Roman Catholic chapel in
England. The importation of foreign velvet,
however, being prohibited in England, it was left
in the custody of the Mansell family, with whom
it remained till the year 1833, when the present
Earl, being written to on the subject by the Very
Reverend the Dean, most generously made a present of it to the church, although he could have
then easily introduced it into England, as the
prohibition no longer exists; and its value is estimated at £300.

This church was the last consecrated of the ten
parish churches in the island, and dedicated to
St. Peter on the 1st of August, 1312, when the
Bishop of Coûtance officiated, accompanied by
the Abbot of Mont St. Michel, the Governors of
Cherbourg, Caen, Havre de Grace, and South-

ampton, also a great assembly of distinguished
individuals, amongst whom were sixteen brothers
of the name of Cornet, who are supposed to have
given their name to the adjoining street—" La
Rue des Cornets," (Horn-street), as also to Castle
Cornet.

There is a fine-toned organ in this church, an
excellent clock which moves four dials, and a
peal of eight bells. Divine service is performed
here three times on Sundays: in French, at ten
o'clock; the garrison service in English at half-
past twelve; and French evening service at half-
past six. Prayers in French are also read every
Wednesday and Friday morning at ten o'clock.

The Markets.

The vegetable market, which is held in an open
square near the town church, is extremely well
supplied with the finest fruit, flowers, and vegetables, that any market can boast of, the only
drawback to which being (on Wednesdays and
Saturdays) the crowded and consequently con-
fused state of the articles for sale, the very profusion of which renders a choice and attention
difficult. This also is, we hope, about to be re-
medied by a market similar to those erected for
fish and meat.

Fish Market.

The fish market, indeed, is admitted by all
strangers to be one of the finest in Europe; about
two hundred feet in length by twenty in breadth,
and upwards of forty in height. The stalls on

which the fish is exposed for sale are forty in number, formed of slabs of finely polished marble, and, being double stalls, are supported on six pillars.

This market is well lighted, by means of windows at each end and of sky-lights in the roof; and it is so well ventilated, and kept so extremely clean, as scarcely to resemble a fish market when cleared at night of its tenants. It is abundantly supplied with fish, particularly in the summer season, when, not only is every stall covered and every corner filled with fresh basket loads of fish, but the adjoining street has frequently a row of small carts and horses laden in readiness for a fresh supply: this is principally in the mackerel season, when the draught is astonishing. Guernsey is noted for its excellent whiting-pollock, turbot, brill, plaice, red and white mullet, john dorey, grey and red gurnet, bream, congor eel, cod, smelts, and sand eels; also of shell fish, lobsters, spider crabs and pound crabs, very cheap, and some of them of an immense size; also, oysters, from September to April, for about eighteen pence per hundred; and the "aumer," *auris marina*, a shell fish in some measure peculiar to these islands, which are very plentiful, and excellent eating when properly dressed. The country people simply fry them, but they should be beaten to render them tender, and stewed in a rich gravy.

The shell of this fish is univalve, with a row of perforations on one side, and, being destitute of protection on the under side, this animal clings to the rocks like the limpet, or to loose stones, from

which, however, they are very easily detached;
and the stranger may collect some specimens of
any size for himself at low tide, on the rocks off
Castle Cornet, or in any of the bays, particularly
at Cobo Bay, and the Vazon Bay, in the Câtel
parish, or at Le Rhé, and the Isle of Lihou.
When cleaned with a little muriatic acid, they
have every variety of hue in the clear mother-of-
pearl which lines the interior, and form a beautiful addition to the conchologist's cabinet.

Meat Market.

The meat market is a very convenient, airy,
and well-planned building, well lighted by sky-
lights in the day time, and with gas lamps by
night. The shops are comfortably fitted up, and
quite distinct one from the other: besides which,
an arcade is set apart for the use of the country
people who are not butchers, and bring their ready
dressed porkers and calves for sale here; they are
hung up in the division to which they belong;
the ten parishes having their names over their
respective line of hooks, so that every purchaser
may know in what parish the meat was fed.
There is a standard weight, a good supply of
fresh water, and the meat is as fine as can be
seen any where.

This market is open every day; but the principal days are Wednesdays and Saturdays. On
Friday, the pork market is always held.

Assembly Rooms.

On one side of the market-square are the Halls,
" Les Halles," appropriated to the use of the

French women, who sell poultry, eggs, and fruit; and, also, where public auctions are held. Over this are the Assembly Rooms, where all public balls, concerts, and exhibitions take place; but they are private property, belonging to a number of island gentlemen; and the assemblies are very select, no strangers, except officers in garrison or of King's ships on the station, can be admitted, but through means of a ticket from a native sub-scriber.

The Royal Court House.

About two centuries ago, public justice was administered in a building which, like those still used in many country towns in England, was both Corn Market and Court House, which by a special ordinance was to be cleared by noon that the market might commence; and after that a Court House was erected near Pollet-street, near a place called from that circumstance " La Plaiderie." This, however, was soon found too small and in-convenient, and the present building was erected in 1799, at an expense of about 7000*l.*, paid by the States, and further improved in 1822. The front elevation is composed of fine square blocks of hewn granite, and the interior is worthy of notice for the regularity and convenience of the different offices, and the good taste displayed in the various embellishments. The lower part of the Court House is divided into the Greffe-office, where all real property transactions and all pro-ceedings of the States and Royal Court are regis-tered; a lesser court where police cases are heard

c

and disposed of, private examinations take place, and where out of term the whole court not unfrequently sits, particularly in the winter season and on days when the number of suitors is small. There is also a retiring room for private consultation on the transacting of any incidental business. The fine circular flight of stone steps lead to the upper or principal court, which has accommodation for about 200 persons besides the court officers. The bailiff, who is chief magistrate, occupies an elevated seat in the centre of the bench; the twelve magistrates, called jurats, on his right and left, according to seniority. Inside the bar, immediately in front of the bailiff, is the table of the greffier or registrar; the crown lawyers, the advocates, the attorney-general and solicitor-general occupying their respective places at the end of the bench. Against the walls are full-length portraits of Daniel de Lisle Brock, the late bailiff, voted by the States in commemoration of numerous public services of the greatest importance rendered at different periods to the island. Next to him the late Admiral Lord de Saumarez, K. C. B., &c. &c., and Rear Admiral of England, a native inhabitant, most deservedly beloved and admired, not only as one of Britain's bravest heroes, but as the warm supporter of every measure that was calculated to benefit his country, as the encourager of every benevolent institution, and by those who best know him as a truly Christian nobleman. On the left is a full-length portrait of Sir John Doyle, K. C. B., Lieutenant-Governor of the island from 1803 to 1817, whose generous and enterprising

spirit in effecting many improvements has been
gratefully remembered by the islanders. A three
quarter-length portrait over one of the doors is
that of the present Lord Seaton, late Sir John
Colbourne, formerly Lieutenant-Governor of the
island.

Opposite the Court House is the first Wesleyan
chapel erected in the island, capable of containing
600 persons. The foundation stone was laid in
1789, by the late celebrated Adam Clarke, LL.D.,
F. R. S., who was one of the first preachers by
whom Methodism was introduced in these islands.
The services are in French: on Sundays at nine
in the forenoon, two in the afternoon, and six in
the evening; on Tuesdays and Thursdays at seven
in the evening.

In the middle of this square is the town residence of the late Lord de Saumarez, and on the
right is Government House, connected with which
are the Government and Inspector of Strangers'
offices, where all arrivals are reported, and passports are obtained (gratis) for France.

The Town Hospital.

For this excellent institution, which stands
immediately below Government House, we are
indebted to the exertions of Mr. Nicholas Dobree,
who first occasioned its establishment and supported it strenuously during his life. It was built
in the year 1742, and the land now belonging to
it was the gift of the Le Mesurier family, who
contributed munificently towards its progress; a
Mr. James Perchard also bestowing no less than

1000*l.* upon its treasury. Over the door, at the side of the large porch, is a representation, cut in stone, of a pelican feeding her offspring with her blood, underneath which is the inscription, "Hôpital de St. Pierre Port, 1742."

The stranger will be struck with the appearances of comfort in every department, with the cleanliness and convenience of the interior, the cheerfulness of the wards, and the perfect good order prevailing every where. A fine open square, with a few old trees, gives an airy and shady walk for the infirm and convalescent; a play-ground also for the children. In the left wing are the wards of the sick, the boys' school-room, the chapel, and the Governor's room; under which is a basement-story, where weaving and other branches of industry are conducted. The centre building, in which is the directors' meeting-room, is appropriated to the men; whilst the right wing, with a separate yard, is devoted to the women and girls. There is another yard, in which are buildings for cooking, brewing, and washing, &c. &c., also a few strong rooms for the insane.

In this establishment are received all such sick or infirm inhabitants as are either in absolute destitution, or incapable of earning their livelihood, all orphan children who have no friends to bring them up, all poor strangers who have met with accidents, or, being too weak to be taken home, are received here, whether British subjects or not; but the latter are paid for by the constables of the Town parish, who levy a separate tax for these emergencies.

A medical attendant is annually elected from amongst the resident surgeons; and experienced nurses are provided for the sick, who are most carefully attended to in every respect. A chaplain is appointed, who visits them constantly, besides a number of lady visitors, who voluntarily attend to the sick and afflicted, providing them with every needful comfort for the body, and with spiritual instruction and consolation.

The healthy inmates are employed in various ways; making mats, nets, mattresses, shoemaking and tailoring, and the women in spinning, mending, washing, knitting, and plain work. There are two very good schools for the children, where they learn both English and French, writing and arithmetic, until they are fit for apprenticeship and service. They are warmly and decently clad, and amply supplied with wholesome food. They are also allowed to visit their friends after service on Sunday afternoon; the men on one Sunday, the women on the other.

There is a house of correction attached to it, where the men are employed in grinding corn at a hand-mill, and breaking stones for roads, and the women in spinning flax, and sewing.

The Hospital is under the direction of a treasurer, vice-treasurer, and six gentlemen, all of whom are elected by the parishioners, and serve one year; half of them going out of office every six months. Besides these, the jurats of the Royal Court, the rector of the parish, all ex-treasurers of the establishment, the procureur of the poor, the churchwardens of the parish, overseers and constables, are ex officio, and allowed to vote at the meetings of directors. Printed reports are annually laid before the public, to which the stranger may refer for more particular information. A fever-ward has been lately added to this establishment, at a cost of 100*l.*

The Public Jail.

This prison, which is immediately behind the Court-House, was erected in 1811, and cost about 11,000*l.* It is a good solid structure, built entirely of blue granite, but smaller than it appears from the exterior, having but little depth, and containing only three lock-up cells for disorderly subjects, which are for the use of the constables, and five debtors' cells on the lower gallery, all of which have fire-places; they are provided with a bedstead, a palliasse, and blankets, by their creditors, but are obliged to find their own bed and furniture: they are unlocked, both in summer and winter, from eight in the morning till sunset, and have a large court to walk in. All the debtors' cells have bell-pulls, communicating with the bed-room of the Governor of the jail, in case of accidents or sickness. The cells for felons and other offenders are in the gallery above that of the debtors, ten in number, eight of which are for men, and two for women.

Mrs. Fry, who visited this jail in September, 1833, observed that the cells for the women were not sufficiently apart from those of the men, as they could easily converse with each other when locked up, and much more so when taking the air, which is not advisable. It is also to be regretted that there is no employment for those who are sentenced to solitary confinement. Drunkards, and boys of disorderly conduct, both in mind and body, would be benefited by a house of correction, where they might be well worked during the day, and placed in solitary confinement during the night.

There is no sick-ward or chapel; but Bibles and religious tracts are provided for the prisoners, and they are visited frequently by their excellent chaplain, the Rev. Henry Benwell.

The Theatre

Is opposite the jail, in exterior like an old storehouse, but well fitted up, and of a tolerable size; not very well attended, though a good company of actors come over every winter for a few months.

St. James's Church.

St. James's Church, which is opposite to the prison, has nothing remarkable in its appearance or interior, being simply fitted up with accommodations for about 1300 persons. The foundation-stone was laid on the 1st day of May, 1817; and in the following year it was consecrated by the Bishop of Salisbury, who had been deputed to perform the ceremony by the Lord Bishop of Winchester. This church was raised partly by subscription, to which the late Lord de Saumarez contributed most munificently, and partly by the sale of pews. The appointment of the minister rests with the proprietors; his salary is 330*l.*

per annum.   The church service is in English
twice on Sunday, at half-past ten in the morning,
and half-past six in the evening.   Prayers are
read every Wednesday and Friday morning, besides a lecture on Wednesday evening.   The sacrament is administered on the first Sunday of
every month.   Perhaps few places in the world, if
any, enjoy so many religious privileges as Guernsey; there is not a day in the week, or an hour in
the Sabbath, where some place of worship is not
open, and where the gospel is soundly and faithfully preached; but I do not enter into the par-
ticulars of each church and chapel, there being
none remarkable for beauty of architecture, or
particularly interesting to the stranger, if we except the last-built church of St. John's, a most
picturesque object from every point; its Gothic
spires rising from the hill-side, in a wooded slope
to the sea, the walk to which *from the New
Ground* will well reward the stranger by its
beauty, and the extensive view that is obtained
from the summit of the hill.   Part of the town
lies immediately beneath, and to the left there is
a sweep of low ground coasting the sea, with the
headland of Mont Crevet and the Vale Castle.
On the right are the wooded grounds of Beau
Sejour and the New Ground; the road winds steeply
down, shaded by hanging trees, under which the
towers of St. John's church are seen as it were in
relief against the channel waters, where Herm
and Jedthou appear in the distance.

St. John's Church.

St. John's is also very tastefully fitted up, and
the windows ornamented with stained glass: the
ceiling is formed of two inclined planes, divided
into panels, by wooden ribs, to which are attached
curved springing pieces, sustained by corbels.
The style is Gothic, and does much credit to the
architect, Mr. Robert Payne. It was built in 1836;
the foundation-stone being laid by Lord De Saumarez. Its endowment consists of a parsonage,
and 17*l.* per annum, secured on rents, together
with the surplus of pew-rents. It is a district
church, having a population of nearly 3000 connected with it. The patronage is vested in five
trustees, of whom the Bishop of Winchester and
Dean of Guernsey are two, the three others, lay-
men. The Rev. Edward Carr is minister. The
church will contain about 800 sittings, when an
addition in progress of erection will have been
completed; of these about 300 are free sittings.
There are two services on Sundays; viz. Morning,
at half-past 10; and Evening, at 6 o'clock. Two
school-houses, in which Sunday, daily, and infant schools are held, have been erected since the
church was built. The church and schools present a most creditable testimony to the liberality
of the Islanders, by whose contributions, with some
aid from Government, they have been erected.

The other churches and chapels will be briefly
noticed in the chapter which gives the places of
worship in St. Peter's Port, and the hours of service.

Elizabeth College.

This is perhaps the most extensive and the
handsomest building in the island. Its form is
that of an oblong square, having a castellated
turret at each angle, with a fifth turret, larger
than the others, in the centre of the building,
from the angles of which rise four spires, which
add greatly to the symmetrical beauty of this
edifice; and from this tower the stranger may
enjoy a most delightful and extensive view of all
the Channel Islands and the coast of France.
The establishment of this College we owe to our
learned Queen Elizabeth. At the time she ascended the English throne the island was in a
deplorable state of ignorance and superstition.
Popery had shaken its scourge over the land,
and persecution, the faggot, and the flame, had
received victims even here. Education was
scarcely known, and the officiating ministers of
religion were of necessity chosen from amongst
strangers. Upon the revival of Protestantism the
parish churches were committed to the care of the
French and Genevese reformed clergy; and with
a view to qualify the islanders for this important
office, and also for other learned professions,
Queen Elizabeth granted a commission, in the
year 1563, to the Governor, Bailiff, Dean, and a
few others, authorizing them to endow a gram-
mar-school, by assigning over to the States a
convent or church, which had formerly belonged
to the society of *Frères Mineurs*, or Grey Friars,
commonly called Cordeliers, with the land adjoin-

ing, including the burial-ground, still called Le Cimétière des Frères. The friars' burial-ground, and about eighty quarters of rent, which had originally been devoted to Popish superstitions, masses, dispensations, &c. &c., were now taken from the Queen's revenue, and applied to the payment of the master's salary.

This institution seems not to have been of much benefit to the island, at least its advantages were never made use of by the inhabitants for many years; indeed not till 1825 did the number of scholars ever exceed twenty-nine; sometimes they were much less, sometimes none at all! No trustees had been appointed to take charge of its landed property; and, consequently, in process of time great part of it was alienated. In 1823 Sir John Colbourne, then Lieutenant-Governor of the island, seconded by the present bailiff, exerted themselves in its favour, and appointed a sub-committee to examine into its circumstances and history. The subject was brought before the States, who resolved on remodelling the statutes of the institution, on erecting a proper building as a college, and introducing an improved system of education not only in this school, but also in all the inferior parish schools. The present college was then commenced, the foundation-stone being laid by Lady Colbourne; and, when finished, was placed under the superintendence of the Lieutenant-Governor and Dean of the island, by virtue of their office, and of thirteen directors, of whom three, namely, the Bailiff, Lieutenant-Bailiff, and the Rector of St. Peter's Port, are permanent directors, but the other ten are appointed only for a limited period, two of them resigning every year, being replaced by others, who are nominated either by the Lieutenant-Governor or the States.

The course of education at this College has since given the greatest satisfaction; and most gratifying testimonials have been afforded by the reports of the public examiners, who come over annually at Midsummer from Oxford, elected for that purpose by the heads of Exeter, Jesus, and Pembroke colleges. Several of its scholars have attained the highest honours at the Universities of Oxford, Cambridge, and Dublin; and receive an education fitting them for every profession, and particularly advantageous to those young men who desire entering either of the Royal Academies at Woolwich, Sandhurst, Haileybury, or Addiscombe.

The fees for education, including the classics, French, mathematics, divinity, commerce, &c. &c. are 12*l.* per annum. Extra charges are made for private tuition, drawing, music, German, Spanish, Italian, dancing, fencing, and drilling; for all of which there are excellent masters in attendance, and the terms are very moderate.

The Principal, who has his residence in the College, receives boarders, who are treated as members of his own family, and partake of all the privileges of the College, at 60*l.* per annum. The Vice-Principal, who lives in the College-house attached to the play-ground, receives pupils in the same manner, at 50*l.*

Amongst other advantages, this College has

EXHIBITIONS, PRIZES, AND MEDAL.

I. An exhibition of 30*l*. per annum, for four years, to the best Classical scholar, native of the bailiwick, or son of a native; founded by the Governor of Guernsey, 1826. Electors: the Examiners and the Principal.

(*In 1836, the office of Governor having been abolished, his late Majesty was graciously pleased to continue the grant, and to allow it to be called the King's Exhibition*).

II. Four exhibitions of at least 20*l*. per annum, for four years, to the best scholars severally, in (1) Divinity and History, (2) Classics, (3) Mathematics, and (4) Modern Languages; founded by subscription, 1826. Electors: the Directors.

(*Prospectuses of these exhibitions may be had at the College Office, States' House, St. Peter's Court, Fountain Street*).

III. An exhibition of 20*l*. per annum, for four years, to the best Classical and Theological scholar; founded by the late Lord de Saumarez, G. C. B., &c., 1827. Electors: the Examiners and the Principal.

IV. Five annual prizes of 2*l*. 2*s*., for Compositions in (1) Latin Prose, (2) Latin Verse, (3) French Prose, (4) English Prose, and (5) English Verse; established by the Directors, 1826.

V. A prize of 2*l*. 2*s*., for a Translation from English into Greek Verse; given by the Principal.

D

VI. Prizes of book tickets, to the amount of 12*l.* 8*s.* annually, from the Directors.

VII. Three prizes of 18*s.*, 14*s.*, and 10*s.*, respectively, for progress in Mathematics; given from 1832 by the Directors.

VIII. A five guinea medal to the best scholar in Geography, Chronology, and Archæology; given from the exhibition fund to subscribers only. Umpires: the Principal and the Vice-Principal.

IX. A prize of five guineas, given in books, to the best Greek scholar, who has not completed his fourteenth year; established from 1831, by Sir William Collings. Umpires: the Principal and the Vice-Principal.

X. Three prizes, each of five guineas, given in books, to the best English, French, and Commercial scholars; established from 1833, by the Directors, from a fund left to the College by the late Eleazar Le Marchant, Esq., Lieut.-Bailiff. Examiners: the Principal, and others appointed by the Directors.

XI. Prizes of books, to the amount of seven guineas, to the best Geographical scholar in each form; given from 1833 by the Principal.

XII. A prize of five guineas, given in books, to the best Theological scholar of the two highest forms; established from 1836, by the Bishop of Winchester. Umpires: the Examiners.

The Vacations are for about two months at Midsummer, two weeks at Christmas, and one at Easter.

Bookseller, publisher, and stationer to Elizabeth

College, Henry Redstone (Commercial Arcade), appointed at Christmas 1842.

The New Cemetery.

This stands on a rising ground, commanding so beautiful a view that it is worthy of a visit. It has been tastefully laid out, but there are not many large or handsome monuments; the principal one is the Mausoleum, in blue granite, erected over the family vault by the heirs of the late Isaac Carey, Esq., of Hauteville.

L'Hyvreuse.

On the New Ground is a public promenade, very near the New Cemetery, which was devoted to public amusements in the year 1782, divided into two parts; the upper ground, which is an open square of fresh green turf, surrounded with a broad gravel walk and clumps of fine trees, from which a beautiful view may be obtained, looking down from the north side over the grounds of Beau Sejour, the seat of Harry Dobree, Esq.; and from the south-west point, close to Castle Carey, which commands one of the finest and most extensive prospects in the island: this is the residence of John Carey, Esq., and has a good collection of paintings, some of which are by the oldest masters. The upper ground serves as a parade to the insular Militia—as a cricket-ground for the students of Elizabeth College; and on the Guernsey fête days, which are principally Easter and Midsummer, when a general review takes place, attracting every merry-making damsel from the ten parishes. The ground is literally thronged with spectators, carriages, equestrians, which latter, however, are restricted to the outer road, and the scene is one of the most enlivened and amusing: even the experienced eye of a military hero might be gratified by the clean and orderly appearance of our native soldiers; their movements are well conducted, and, considering that they are drilled altogether but four times a year, it is wonderful how very well they go through the different evolutions. The lower part of this ground is thickly wooded, with a broad gravel walk, over which the arching branches shadowing fall, giving a cool resting-place in the hottest summer day; and when all is as quiet round as if the town and the busy world were altogether afar of, only a few nurses with playful children, or a solitary wanderer with a book, may be found on ordinary days. The time is gone by when this was the fashionable evening lounge, with a bugle band from Fort George, to give a plausible excuse for the consequent flirtations. The Grange Road, without any of the New Ground attractions, has become the favourite walk, where butterfly beaux for ever flit round our Guernsey lilies.

From L'Hyvreuse there are several pleasant walks and shady lanes, where few steps intrude; one leads to the pretty village of St. Jacques, and from thence to the Câtel Road, branching off in several directions to the farthest points of the island.

The Grange Road

Is that which leads from the town to the country by St. James's Church and Elizabeth College: the stranger will not require directions for noticing the number of delightful residences on either side the whole way up. This, as I before observed, is the fashionable walk, at least it is the favourite resort of the idle and the gay, but also frequented by those who belong to neither of these classes, from this road being the principal outlet from town to the several parishes of Câtel, St. Andrew's, St. Martin's, St. Peter's-in-the-Wood, &c. &c. If you are going to what, *of course,* you will wish to see—Fort George, then, instead of following the straight line which runs towards the Câtel, turn to the left, and in the winding way up to Petite Marche and Colbourne Place, not only will pleasant dwellings and beautiful gardens open upon you at every step, but you will most likely meet the élite of the island—the lilies of our Guernsey homes, radiant in the beauty of youth and health, as many and as fair flowers as you will find in any country. At Colbourne Place the road again branches off to St. Andrew's on the right, to the town, by Mount Durand (a very steep hill), on the left; straight on lies the way to Fort George, down to a pretty valley, then up a hill-side by a beautiful road, and as the Fort comes in sight, one of the most splendid views the eye ever beheld bursts upon you.

Fort George

Was built between the years 1782 and 1826, finished under the auspices of General Sir John Doyle, the Lieutenant-Governor. It is a regular fortification of considerable strength, with a signal station corresponding with that of Castle Cornet. Immediately below the hill, and breaking the descent, are terraces, houses, and shrubberies meeting the town of St. Peter's, which stretches out in a semicircle, and slopes off to the Vale, St. Michael's Castle, Mont Crevet, St. Sampson's. Castle Cornet stands in front of the harbour; the islands of Herm and Jedthou about three miles of; Serk, on the right, more distant; and Alderney on the horizon towards the north, with the Casket Rocks on one side, and the Coast of France, seen at intervals, on the other. The stranger may wander round the Fort by the Artillery Barracks at Belvidere, and coasting this promontory by way of the tracks down its rocky sides, will return again and again unweared to this lovely and quiet spot, to watch the tides of the Channel sea in all its moods.

The islands of Serk and Herm add considerably to the beauty of Guernsey, and give her greatly the advantage in point of sea-scenery over her sister island Jersey; not only because they break the monotony of the ocean, and unconsciously fill our mind with ideas, by raising expectation of something unknown which we long to explore; but also, because they really do not, as most such things do, "keep the promise to the eye, to break it to the heart." You may look at these craggy cliffs of Serk, round which perhaps the perpetual currents are rushing in a foamy chain, and think you shall like to run over and peep at its inhabitants, &c. If you do so, you will be surprised to find *how much* there is to see. That barren-looking, desolate island, has the loveliest valleys, the most splendid caves, the pleasantest cottages, and as comfortable lodgings as you can wish for, with ample amusement for a week at least. I have spent *months* there—months of unwearied delight, and always left it half unexplored, to look forward to another visit. The only guide-book is "The Recollections of Serk"*; it points out the curiosities of the place, and gives a brief account of its early history and romantic first settlement.

CHAPTER II.

ST. SAMPSON'S—THE VALE—CROMLECHS, &C.

HAVING noticed all that is most interesting within the boundaries of the Town parish, we shall do the same by each of the other parishes separately and in succession, commencing with that of

ST. SAMPSON'S,

but leaving it to the good pleasure of the stranger to choose his own road thither; and, as objects of interest are not the same to every mind, he may

* Published and sold by H. Redstone, Commercial Arcade, Guernsey.

thus visit whichever has most claim upon his attention, which, with the assistance of a map, and
the civility he will surely find in asking his way,
renders any particular guidance unnecessary, if
not intrusive.   The usual road to St. Sampson's
is by the sea side; there are three omnibuses,
plying constantly between the harbour there and
St. Peter's Port; the stand is at the Town church,
and the fare five-pence; but the walk is so beautiful, the stranger will doubtless prefer it.

He may at first be somewhat discouraged on
entering the narrow and frequently *dirty* Pollet-
street, which will, I doubt not, be improved in
the course of a few years, as it forms a most dis-
agreeable and unworthy communication between
the two principal parishes; but after proceeding
a short distance, he may remark on the left a fine
old house, called the "Plaiderie," formerly the
Royal Court House, and on the right are the
Public Baths.   Only a little farther, passing the
noisy ship-builders' yards, he will be repaid for
his two minutes' walk through the Pollet by
coming out upon the

Esplanade,

a marine walk, constructed in 1826 on a breakwater, which was absolutely necessary for the
protection of property, the spring-tides being extremely violent on this coast under a south-east
or north-east gale.   A battery, mounting four
guns, is at the end of the Esplanade, called the
"Sallérie," running out on a small headland,
which gives shelter to fishing-boats and skiffs in

a south wind; this name, which is also given to
the adjoining street, is derived from a royal salt-
ing-house, which stood here some centuries ago
when the island was a mere fishery. From this
battery the view is most beautiful at all times; at
sunrise, on a summer morning, who would not
leave his idle dreams to stand upon the sea-shore,
and breathe the pure life-quickening breeze, or
watch the uprising of the glorious sun over the
Isle of Serk, which lies in the purple distance?
each little wave is crowned with a wreath of glittering spray, and chase each other along the rapid
tide, fretting against the dark rocks scattered so
thickly everywhere. The eye wanders over the
whole sweep of the fine bay, pausing at the Islands of Herm and Jedthou, immediately in front,
then at the old Vale Castle on the extreme left, or
the Island Castle Cornet on the right, which is
most likely studded with signals, answering those
of many a noble ship now proudly bearing her
full sails as she presses on to the *Home* Harbour.
It is a worthy sight to rise and see, yet scarcely
less lovely at the sunset hour, and perhaps *more*
beautiful yet when a south-east gale is rising and
a fearful swell convulses the whole Channel.
There is only one spot better worth going to in
the whole island, that is, on the very point of
Pleinmont. Stranger! if you love the sea in its
wrath—if your heart bounds at the terrible sport
of giant waves, lashed into madness by a stormy
wind, go to Pleinmont; but as you stand in safety
there, breathe a prayer to the Ruler of the winds
and waves, that no misguided ship be cast within

the tide, which would dash them on the Hanois Rocks beneath you. Many a life has perished there!

To return however to the Esplanade, we must notice the battery beyond the Sallérie, which, with its martello tower, is called Hougue à la Père; this is the spot where executions take place (a most rare occurrence). These martello towers, of which there are fifteen round the island, were constructed at the commencement of the revolutionary war. No object of particular interest will now detain the stranger in his sea-side walk until he arrives at

St. Sampson's Church,

the most ancient of religious edifices on the island. When Childebert of France bestowed the bishopric of these islands on St. Sampson, Bishop of Dol, in the sixth century, the spot where St. Sampson landed was called by his name, and a small chapel founded and dedicated to him, which having fallen to decay, the present church was erected on the same spot, and consecrated in 1111, by Roger, Bishop of Coûtance. The pointed arch at one end of this church is remarkable as a specimen of ancient architecture. The present rector, both of this parish and of the Vale, is the Reverend William Chepmell.

St. Sampson's Harbour

Is the only one in the island besides that of St. Peter's Port; and though the latter monopolizes the whole of the foreign trade, and the greatest part of the local trade, consisting in the exportation of potatoes, potato spirit, apples, cider, corn, cows, &c.; yet this harbour is daily rising in importance. The haven is a safe and commodious one, provided with a quay, warping-buoys, and beacons; having also a breakwater, which stems the tide to the south-east, so that, in point of security, vessels ride out a gale with less injury in the heaviest storms than they do in the Port of St. Peter's. Ships are being built round this harbour, which has storehouses and docks; and all shipments of Guernsey granite are made from hence. The quarries from which the principal supply is obtained are very near the harbour: excellent gray granite, forming the best paving stones in the world; or, as a paviour once said, " Guernsey stone is a very bad pavement for a poor man—it never wears out:" and it has an advantage even over the noted Aberdeen granite of above 19 lbs. in the cubic feet, having greater density and solidity of substance, for

Aberdeen granite weighs 2690 oz. per cubic foot.
Guernsey paving stone, 2999 oz.   ditto.

The usual prices of Guernsey stone rendered alongside of the vessel are as follows:—

Spalls or chippings, of all sizes, to be broken for the purpose of Macadamizing roads . . . } 1s. 8d. per ton,

The same broken up and ready for laying . . . . } 4s. 0d. —

Paving stones . . . . 7s. 0d. —

The freights to London vary according to the demand for stone, and the number of vessels offering from 7s. to 9s. per ton.

A late Lord Mayor of London rose to fortune
from his having been employed as a stone-cutter
at St. Sampson's. He came to Guernsey in some
distress, having left England for a youthful frolic,
and, in order to support himself, he obtained employment as journeyman stone-cutter to a respectable farmer at the Vale. Several years after this
he returned again to London, and whilst strolling
about unoccupied, he accidentally came to a street
which was being paved with Guernsey stone; ob-
serving that the workmen were laying it down in
a very clumsy manner, he pointed out how they
might do it better. Whilst so engaged, he at-
tracted the notice of the contractor, who immediately hired him as his foreman. He subsequently
became contractor himself,—amassed considerable wealth,—was elected Alderman, and finally
elevated to the highest civic dignity, being chosen
Lord Mayor.

This was quite unknown in the island, until
Sir John Doyle, then Lieutenant-Governor of
Guernsey, dining one day at the Mansion-House,
was asked by the Alderman next to him how his
old master was, mentioning his name.   The General was surprised, and repeated the question,—
" Your master!"   " Yes," replied the worthy
Alderman, " the master for whom I worked as a
journeyman stone-cutter in St. Sampson's harbour, when I was a wild young man; pray remember me kindly to him as William Staines,
and say, that I shall be most happy to receive
him in London."

Ivy Castle.

This ruin, for it is nothing else, lies near the town, and not far from the battery of Hougue à la Perè; it was formerly called Le Château des Marais, but since its walls have crumbled under the hand of time, and a mantle of ivy has been thrown over it, the name has changed to Ivy Castle. It was erected in 1036, on the following occasion:—

Robert Duke of Normandy, surnamed Le Diable, having collected a considerable fleet and army for the purpose of assisting Edward the Confessor, who laid claim to the English crown after the death of Canute, met with a violent storm off this coast on his way to England; his fleet was scattered—many of his followers perished; and he, with the remainder, was compelled to seek shelter in Guernsey.

They came to an anchor at the north side of the island in a bay which has ever since been called L'Ancresse Baie—or the bay of anchorage, and landed safely. Being very hospitably treated by the inhabitants, and principally by the abbots and monks of St. Michael, he gave them several proofs of his gratitude, particularly in leaving behind him several skilful engineers, whom he directed to construct fortresses and improve the Vale Castle, so as to defend the monks and inhabitants from the depredations of those lawless pirates and freebooters who, at that time, infested the Channel Sea, and frequently made inroads upon the defenceless islanders, destroying their lives and pro-

E

perty without resistance. One of the fortresses then erected, was this castle; the other a fortification at Jerbourg, in the parish of St. Martin. Le Château des Marais appears to have been doubly walled and moated; the outer wall encloses a space of about four acres, and has a ditch round it. There is also another ditch between this wall and the inner ballium. On the approach of an enemy both ditches could be filled immediately from an adjacent rivulet of great power, and as readily dried up again by means of sluices. There are few remains of the original building, but the spot is still picturesque and interesting. It belongs to the Governor of the Island for the time being.

THE VALE PARISH.

The parish was once curiously divided by the encroachments of the sea, at the north-west point, at " Le Grand Havre," where a tract of land containing eight hundred vergées was completely submerged until wrested from its dominion by the persevering efforts of General Sir John Doyle. The Braye du Vale is now under cultivation, and good houses are rising fast where the ocean rolled not many years ago.

The Vale Castle

Stands on the headland north of St. Sampson's Harbour, forming an interesting and picturesque object. In the tenth century, a party of monks emigrated or were expelled from the monastery of Mount St. Michael, in Normandy, and took refuge on this almost unknown island, where (whatever might have been their reasons for settling here) they certainly made a rapid progress in civilizing the inhabitants and confirming the Christian religion amongst them. Finding themselves greatly exposed to the attacks of the lawless pirates who infested the channel, who frequently landed to plunder the defenceless inhabitants, carrying off corn and cattle " à volonté," the monks erected this fortress near the most thickly-populated village, and it was then large and strong enough to receive and defend all the inhabitants, with their goods and cattle.

This fortress they named after their former dwelling — St. Michael the Archangel. And though little now remains of the ancient castle, except the outer walls and ramparts, yet it evidently was a place of considerable strength, and admirably situated both as a watch tower and fortress. The view from it is very beautiful.

Vale Church.

This church was erected in 1117, close to the ruins of the Abbey of St. Michael, which was a monastery built by the same monks who raised the fortress of the Vale Castle. When Robert of Normandy left the island, after his shipwreck and hospitable reception by the inhabitants, he bestowed all the land on the north-west coast upon the monks, including part of the Câtel and St. Saviour's parishes, by the title of the Fief or

Manor of St. Michael, empowering the abbot also to hold a feudal court to decide all causes, civil as well as criminal. This church did not belong to the abbey, but was built by the parishioners, and consecrated on the 29th of September, 1117, by Alexander le Revingier, Bishop of Coûtances, the Abbot of St. Michael's, the Hermit of Herm, the Honorable Dame Martine du Val, Abbesse de Caen, and many other noble personages, who likewise made great gifts to the church, and who heartily joined in the consecration service, of which some parts are worth recording.

When the multitude were on their knees, both within and without the holy place, the bishop caused a sea-faring boy to mount the pinnacle of the temple, having a sponge full of water and oil, who, at the command of the bishop, squeezed out half the sponge on the pinnacle and the other half on the cemetery, and then the bishop pronounced his blessing upon the church, dedicating it to "St. Michael the Angel and Archangel," which being said, a cock was planted on the pinnacle, in token that the pastor was to watch over his flock as a cock does over his hens; and besides this, the silken ensign of the noble Remont Sauvage, Governor of the castle and parish, floated over the church, and there were great rejoicings and feastings during forty days.

The ivied wall on one side of the churchyard is part of the ancient abbey, as also some pointed arches on the south wall. Opposite the western door there is a Cromlech or Druids' altar, of which there are several in this parish.

CROMLECHS *at the Vale.*

These Druidical remains consist chiefly of broad flat slabs of granite, placed on high in a horizontal posture upon others fixed in the ground, being altars on which the ancient Druids sacrificed and made prodigious fires on Mayday eve.

The finest Cromlech in Guernsey is called the *Druids' Temple,* and stands on an eminence near l'Ancresse Bay and the Vale Church. It is composed of five cumbent stones, decreasing in size from about twenty to ten tons in weight, covering an area twenty-nine feet long and nearly twelve feet wide. The drifting sands had once completely covered this monument of antiquity, and it was only accidentally discovered in 1812. The remains of several antique earthen vessels were then dug up, and an immense quantity of human teeth and bones, some of them bearing evident marks of fire, which is sufficient proof of its having been a sepulchre, if not devoted to the purpose of human sacrifice. The sands are again gathering round it, and possibly, in a few years, it will have disappeared, unless it is secured by a wall or some kind of protection.

There is another fine Cromlech at Paradise, near Bordeaux harbour, in this parish, consisting of two immense flat stones lying north-east and south-west, inclining towards the former direction, and supported by a number of smaller ones. This is the most perfect Cromlech uncovered, the land round it having been purchased by a private individual for the purpose of preserving it.

A third Cromlech, of smaller size, stands midway on the common, between Montemar Height and Vale Church.

A fourth, in a field near St. Sampson's, called Le Champ de l'Autel, which has been preserved, although the land all round it was purchased for quarrying, owing to a superstition which led the seller of the property to warn the new proprietor, that, if ever he removed or injured the altar, he would never be happy or prosperous. This superstitious feeling is confirmed in the peasants by a singular coincidence which occurred some years ago, and which they invariably relate to strangers.

In a field about half a mile from the church, still called "Le Courtil du Roc qui sonne," or "Field of the Sounding Stone," there was a large stone, supposed to be a Celtic remains, which, on being struck, emitted a clear, hollow, ringing sound, and which was considered as sacred. But about forty years ago, the owner of the field, being on the point of building a house, determined to make use of the idle stone; when, in spite of all warning, and to the great terror of the neighbours, he unscrupulously broke it up, and used it for supports to his door and window openings. No immediate judgment fell upon the sacrilegious offender; but in less than twelve months his new house was burnt to the ground. He built it up again; and a second time, in a most unaccountable manner, it shared the same fate. Then, resolving not to hazard a third attempt, he sold the stones, and shipped them off for England; but still the same fatality attended them: the vessel foundered at sea, and all on board perished. So the Guernseyman is, *fortunately*, fully persuaded that it is a perilous and evil thing to touch a Cromlech, otherwise they had all long ere this been in cottage walls and church gateways.

The Logan, or balancing stone, called "Le Roc Balan," has been found in Guernsey; but unfortunately was blasted, unawares, by some men employed in an adjoining quarry.

In the Bay Du Croc, at the north-west point, there is an immense heap of such large stones, evidently of Celtic formation; some of them must weigh full one hundred tons; and in this neighbourhood many antique remains have been excavated, such as cleavers of fine marble, edged and pointed, similar to those which the Druids used for flaying their victims. When they were first found, some of the country-people took them for *thunderbolts!*

L'Ancresse Common,

Which surrounds the church, is made use of as a race-course. The races take place every June, for which her Majesty gives a handsome silver cup, and other considerable plates are contested for by the island horses, whose breed has greatly improved lately, and are by no means discreditable to their proprietors. There are plates open for strangers, and the usual concluding amusements of donkey races, foot races, &c., &c., amongst the lower orders, during two days, when, tents and booths being erected, and the whole

island swarming to witness the contest, the
scene is one of great animation and interest for
those who enjoy it.

There is nothing more to be seen in this parish;
but a pleasant walk towards Cobo Bay brings the
stranger into the adjoining parish of the Câtel.

There is a parish school, and dissenting
schools and chapel in every parish; the latter,
we are sorry to say, by far more numerously
attended than the former. The chapels belong
generally to the Wesleyan Methodists, who are
so very zealous in their labours that it is greatly
to be regretted their efforts are not made on
behalf of their mother church of England.

CHAPTER III.

ST. MARY OF THE CASTLE, OR THE CATEL PARISH,

Is bounded by St. Andrew's, St. Saviour's and the
Vale parishes, and is one of the largest in the
island, joining St. Peter's Port on the north-west.

The stranger, when setting out for a walk over
the Câtel Parish, must take the Grange Road,
and continue straight on where it branches off
at Choisie House, the residence of the late Lieut.-
Governor Sir James Douglas. He will soon pass
an ivied archway of Saxon origin, which leads to
an old building at present inhabited by a farmer,
but which, from its extent and evident antiquity,
was doubtless either a convent or the residence of
some manorial lord. The primitive buildings

formed an extensive quadrangle, entered by two massive Saxon portals: the outbuildings of which, and the garden wall, bear the same stamp of antiquity.

Ivy Gate, as it is called, now forms the entrance to a group of modern houses, called De Beauvoir. The short and direct way to the Câtel Church from hence is, to continue this road, turn up the Rohais Hill, and the church is seen on the summit of the rising ground, commanding a splendid view. The lower parishes on one side, the wooded environs of the town on the other, the ocean beyond, upon which the Casket Rocks, the islands of Alderney and part of Herm are seen resting in softened hues upon the deep waters, with a distant outline of France on the horizon, whilst the broken ground of this old churchyard fills up the foreground, with interesting remains of that ancient castle upon whose ruins the church now stands.

History is somewhat obscure upon the point; but in the early ages when the fertility and beauty of this island were scarcely known, it was frequently invaded by the piratical Danes and other barbarous nations, who ravaged the country and pillaged the defenceless inhabitants; and a pirate chieftain, called Le Grand Sarazin or Le Grand Geoffrey, took possession of this height, upon which he erected a castle or fortress, and made forays at his pleasure over the island.

William Duke of Normandy, previous to his invasion and conquest of England, took the state of these islands into consideration, and immedi-

ately sent one of his generals, Sampson D'An-
neville, to expel the pirates from their stronghold.

This after some difficulty he at length effected.
Le Grand Sarazin was killed or fled, and his castle
pulled down, upon the site of which the present
church was built and dedicated, in commemoration of the event, to "Our Lady of the Deliverance of the Castle."

The consecration of the church took place on
the 25th of August, 1203, by the Abbot and
Prior of the Vale and Parish of St. Michael the
Archangel, who was authorized to do so by the
Bishop of Coûtances, and it was dedicated to
"Our Lady of the Deliverance, the Mother of our
Lord and Saviour Jesus Christ," in the midst of
a great assembly, who made large gifts, presents,
and offerings to the holy place, both in gold and
silver, as a token of gratitude for their release
from their tyrannical pirates, and acknowledgment of the favour bestowed upon them by Almighty God.   The dedication prayer, which has
been handed down through an old local MS., is
worthy of record:—"For when the Abbot of St.
Michael's had ordered the great banner to be
hoisted on the pinnacle of the temple, and when
the multitude had fallen on their knees, both
within the temple and also without in the churchyard, he said—

"Happy temple! may God bless thee, and
keep thee from all evil and peril! and in His Holy
and venerable Name, I bless, dedicate, and conse-
crate thee for His Holy Service, in the Name of

the Father, the Son, and the Holy Ghost; and thou shalt bear the name of Our Lady of the Deliverance, Mother of Our Lord and Saviour Jesus Christ; and may the same and like benediction be upon this churchyard, and the blessed sepulchral earth of faithful Christians, both male and female! praying that all those who may be buried in thee, and in thy holy blessed sepulchral garden, of which the Saviour of the world is gardener, may have grace to rise again at the end of the world, on the last day, to the resurrection of an eternal and most happy life, and be in the company of the elect of God in celestial glory, with his holy angels; praying also, that His Holy Word and His Holy Sacraments may be faithfully administered there, to the great salvation and profit of the bodies and souls both of the pastors and people; and that each testator and testatrix may bear recollection of thee in their earthly goods and in their wills, that they may get good by it; praying the Almighty Creator and Conductor of heaven and earth, that He may keep, protect, and defend thee from all kinds of evils, inconveniences and injuries; from thunderbolts, thunders and lightnings; from rough and violent winds, and all enemies visible and invisible, both in time of peace and time of war." And they all with one pure voice answered—" Amen."

"Then there was great feasting and rejoicing for the space of forty days; all the ensigns of the island were displayed, the bells, organs, drums, and other instruments sounding continually. There was also distributed bread to the amount of

sixty-seven quarters of wheat, twenty fat oxen,
and twenty fat cows, and one hundred head of
small cattle, with eight tuns of cider and six tuns
of wine.   Then they departed thanking God for
having granted them grace to see so holy a work
begun and completed."

It is remarkable that the north and east walls
of this church appear more ancient than the rest,
and of a different structure, wherein some stones
are still seen projecting, with a hole at the end,
and other marks of strong gates having been
there.

A few years back, when this church was under-
going repair, part of the plaster on the north wall
fell off and discovered traces of a fresco painting;
it was carefully picked away, and three different
paintings discovered more or less perfect, but only
the largest and middle one is at all distinct at
present.   The subject of this is involved in
obscurity; there are three figures on horseback
apparently hunting, from their having hawks on
their wrists, and a forest may be denoted by the
tree which stands between them and three im-
perfect skeletons, the centre one enveloped in a
mantle.

The only faint light which can be thrown upon
this, is gathered from the Journal de Coûtances,
which, in relating the discovery of a vault in an
ancient chapel near Coûtances, and the finding of
three skeletons in a peculiar position, refers to an
old tradition which had been preserved amongst
them.

Three "Seigneurs" de Coûtances, brothers, of

the name of Dugas, renowned throughout the country for their irreligion and depravity, went out a hunting on horseback, on Easter Sunday, in the forest of Lessay. At the moment that the sacrament of the mass was celebrated, and the bell tolled at the elevation of the Host, a skeleton rose up miraculously before them; and after uttering in a sepulchral voice this awful warning, " *I was once what you are, but you will soon be what I am,*" disappeared suddenly. The three horses fell on their knees before the apparition, and threw their riders to the ground, who, terrified and conscience smitten, made a solemn vow to God that they would turn from their evil ways, and build a church or chapel if they were spared to return in safety to their dwelling. Some days after this the chapel of St. Michael was founded by them, and it was there the three skeletons were found. There is a singular resemblance between this legend and the painting in St. Mary's church, but nothing more is known about them as yet. Some antiquarian may possibly visit the spot and find the broken clue; at any rate the remains are curious and worthy of inspection. They may be seen any day on application at the cottage near the gate, where the keys of the church are kept. The present Rector of this parish is the Reverend James Maingy.

Foulon Road.

I have conducted the stranger out of town by the shortest and usual road, but not by the *prettiest*. If, after passing Ivy Gate, he takes the

first turn to the left, it will lead him by the Foulon
Road to the Croix au Bailiff Road, and here, instead of the common-place irregular cottages of
the Rohais, which has but one or two redeeming
gentlemanly residences, and is, besides, *over-built*,
he may dip into a pleasant valley, and rise up out,
of the winding way to enjoy an extensive prospect,
and a quiet walk to the Câtel Church.

I mention this to you, stranger, because I hope.
you are not one of those mercurial travellers who
run a race against time, resolved to see all you·
possibly can see in so many given hours, and then
start off again about as wise as you were before.·
I hope you are come really to explore our little
island, and learn to love it; you will not find out
all its worth on the *highway;* and I should like
to make you acquainted with better things even
than public buildings.

If, therefore, you have an eye to see, a heart to
feel the beautiful, if you love a quiet walk amid
nature's mysteries, and care to turn aside out of
the beaten track of ordinary pedestrians, I would
ask you to come again up the Croix au Bailiff
Road, or turn from the Câtel Church, taking the
road *opposite* its churchyard-gate, and when you
reach the pretty cottage which is covered with
clematis, and roses, and myrtle, up and over its
very roof, then turn down the lane on the *left*, if
you *come from* the Croix au Bailiff (there are
three lanes near each other on the left; the one I
mean is in the middle). It seems to lead only to
a farm-yard, *but go on*, it passes through, and
twists and winds on the skirts of the Ponchez

estate, arched over all the way by pleasant rust-
ling trees, which open here and there their leafy
screen to let the merry sunbeams just dance
through. It is a haunted lane: if you are afraid
of unfleshed spirits, you must not walk this way
in the dark; I could *tell*, though I will not *write*,
many a tale of witchcraft and wonder, which are
said to have happened hereabouts. Presently,
you will pass a little purling brook, where a group
of cattle may be pausing to drink on their way
home from the fields; and as you ascend the up-
ward path, you may be told that on the right-
hand hedge-side grow the sweetest and earliest
primroses, violets, and blue bells in all the country
round. I envy any one the pleasure of emerging
for the first time from those shadowy trees, and
catching a glimpse of the sea, particularly when
a little further on you turn a sharp corner, and
the lovely valley of King's Mills is seen beneath
you—the Vazon Bay beyond—Richmond—Le Reè
Barracks dotting the coast, and above all the ocean
glowing under a sunset sky. It is worth while
resting on the bank just here, to watch the curling
smoke rising up from a cottage embedded in the
wood below, and to listen to the evening hymn
which trills out from a hundred little throats;
perhaps too you will hear the distant shout of
some returning labourers, or the deep lowing of
the mother-cow, or a belated overladen bee will
pass by humming drowsily, and hindered on his
way by his accumulated wealth. The rich sunlight too is tinting the landscape with a thousand

hues; and will not this reward you for an extra walk?

But as you are so far, suppose you proceed and walk through Woodlands*, which is close by. It is one of the largest and most beautiful estates on the island; even making allowance for my partial praise of my own dear home, you will find it worth visiting. The house is not remarkable, except for its old irregular appearance; but the grounds have much varied scenery, and (for Guernsey) extensive woodland, in which many rare plants and shrubs are growing luxuriantly.

A *magnolia grandiflora*, thirty feet in height, and eight feet in girth, blossoming every year, is in itself a powerful testimony to the climate of Guernsey, although its unusual growth is attributed to the Holy Well near which it stands. The *hydrangea hortensa* and *verbena tryphylla* flourish here as if in their native soil; and a species of *syringa* from Constantinople, with long pendent clusters of white flowers. The spice plant, or *calycanthus*, may be seen growing from seven to eight feet high, which, twining round a laurel, is covered with rich dark clustering flowers, fragrant and tasting like cloves. The Guernsey lily (*amaryllis sarniensis*) runs wild in the wood, near the haunted cottage of the Domaillerie, and, in the month of September, the bright scarlet flowers are found, radiant with the glittering gold dust sprinkled over its leaves, and

* The seat of Colonel Lane.

many of the stalks bear from seven to nine bells. It is on this estate the famous seedling apple called "Le Pomme Susanne," or Mollet Pippin, was raised, and so named after a former proprietor, who left a valuable orchard of upwards of fifty different choice sorts.

But to return to the Holy Well beneath the magnolia, there is a tale* connected with that huge mis-shapen stone near it, and the little cottage on the opposite side of the wood, which is scarcely seen from the thick foliage of surrounding trees, and the profusion of ivy and honeysuckle which creep over its walls.

It is a haunted place, which I have known stout workmen refuse to pass after nightfall, and no Guernsey person would live there upon any terms; so it has fallen into decay, and the rats and the bats hold almost undisturbed possession of the Domaillerie.

If you pay it a visit, walk on through the grove which overhangs it, and enter the field at the end of the avenue—the Tuzet Field—from the top of which you look down at the pretty village of King's Mills, winding through a wooded valley; there is the Vazon Bay once more, with Houmet Tower on one side, Le Reè and Richmond on the other; a beautiful expanse of ocean; at the same time, an equally fine landscape of hill and dale, woodland and furze-fields, and the meeting parishes of St. Andrew's and St. Saviour's are seen as you turn round towards the east.

* The Domaillerie Cottage, see Appendix.

F 3

You should come here when the last crimson
light of sunset is fading on the ocean, and the
mists of evening are rising from the valley; and
if you love flowers, and are a botanist, you will
possibly find abundance of the lovely "Lady's
Tresses" (*neottia spiralis*) scattered at your feet;
this field is famous for them. Now, either get
over the hedge towards the sea, and cross the only
two fields which lie between you and the village,
or else go down into the meadow, and from thence
pass into the old Groignet estate, which is well
worth walking over. This will bring you equally
to King's Mills, of which I shall say more hereafter; only as every one may not choose to follow
me through my favourite lane, I must go back
to the church and proceed in a more orderly
manner, from thence down the road which runs
along the churchyard, and opposite the *lower gate*
there is a pretty lane leading to

The Country Hospital,

situated in a valley below the church, immediately
behind the parsonage-house; it was built in 1753,
and though badly situated in such low ground, is
commodious and well kept, having about fifty-
two vergées of good land attached to it for the
maintenance of its inmates, who are employed in
its cultivation, and thus enjoy the advantages of
constant fresh air and exercise. This Institution
receives the destitute and infirm of all the country
parishes, also two-thirds of those orphans and
widows who are left by soldiers dying in garrison
here. The stranger will be pleased with the

cleanliness and order of the interior; particularly with the quiet comfort of the sick ward, which looks out upon a sunny garden, where fruit and flowers afford refreshment to the poor sufferers. The children have nurseries and schools, and Divine service is performed gratuitously by each of the country ministers in turn: besides which, the children, and those who are able to do so, attend morning and afternoon service at the church.

From the Country Hospital the stranger will emerge into the lower Câtel Road, continuing which he will soon come to a carrefour where four roads meet, and Saumarez, the country residence of the late Lord de Saumarez, may be observed on the right. Turning to the left, which leads to King's Mills, the first house you pass is

The Haye du Puits,

one of the antiquities of the island. It belongs to the Le Marchant family, and bears upon its ivied walls and turret roof the stamp of other days; here it was that our fugitive Prince, Charles the Second, took refuge, when he passed through these islands on his way to France after the death of his father. It is a great pity that the road has so remorsely been cut through the shrubbery, and destroyed the seclusion of this monastic-looking dwelling.

St. George.

The estate of St. George, belonging to John Guille, Esq., the present bailiff of the island, is next on the road to King's Mills, and here may

still be seen a few ruins of the old chapel of St.
George, which belonged to the Abbey of St.
Michael, and was presented to the parish by an
ancestor of Col. Guille for a public school.

There is also an ivied well, surmounted by a
cross, called "The Holy Well of St. George*,"
the pure waters of which were in great repute
in former times as a never-failing remedy for
swellings, and various affections of the limbs,
known as "*le mal de Fontaine;*" indeed they are
still believed in, and used by some of the country
people, with whom it is customary to draw this
water in secret, depositing a small piece of money
in the niche at the foot of the cross, as an offering
to the patron saint. Superstition has invested
this spot with many terrors, and haunted the
beautiful shrubbery with a number of fanciful
apparitions; even now the peasant child passes
fearfully along the road after night-fall, expecting
to see the fiery head of St. George's charger. But
there is another property attached to this well
which may not be generally known. That if a
maiden visits this well *fasting* and in *silence* on
nine successive mornings, carefully depositing a
piece of silver in the niche as an offering to the
saint, she is assured of matrimony within nine
times nine weeks; and by looking into the well
with an earnest desire to behold the image of the
intended husband, *his face* will appear mirrored
in the water. It was formerly practised, and when
the person was ascertained, the damsel certified his

* *See* "Legend of St. George's Well."

name to the priest, who then summoned him before St. George, and, as destined by Heaven, they were solemnly united.

Adjoining the chapel of St. George was a cemetery which boasted of many valuable relics, and was famous for wonder-working miracles; but the following record is the best worth preserving:—

When St. George was in the height of his reputation, and his well the resort of many a childless wife and unrequited lover, one of his votaries, the only and beloved child of an aged couple, suddenly disappeared both from home and from chapel, without the least clue to the cause of her absence.

She had been a devout and constant attendant at the saint's shrine, and though many persons had remarked her melancholy bearing, the heavy eye and languid step of sorrow, though she had for some time been seemingly estranged from her betrothed, and often surprised in tears, yet no one was prepared for the dreadful discovery of her lifeless body near the Hanois Rocks at Roquaine Bay.

The body was found so mangled that it was evident she did not destroy *herself;* and this terrible shock broke the hearts of her parents, who in a few months slept beside their murdered child in the cemetery of St. George.

No one was convicted, no one even was suspected of the deed; for poor Marie was greatly beloved, and so kind, so good, so gentle, that conjecture was baffled in every attempt to discover the murderer. But from that time the cemetery was a

scene of horrors; every night at a certain hour
the most piteous cries were heard, apparently proceeding from Marie's tomb, and a ghastly human
figure wandered about terrifying the beholder almost to madness. This continued for years, many
years. It was so long ago, that old men told
their grandchildren the story "of the beautiful
girl whose spirit haunted the churchyard of St.
George;" when one day it happened that a grave
was opened so close to Marie's that some dry
bones were thrown up, which several of the by-
standers supposed might be *hers*.

One and another handled these bones; an old
man who had been Marie's lover was there, and
he also took them in his hand, but the moment
he did so, a cry of horror broke from him—a
bitter cry which thrilled through the group—for
a stream of blood oozed out of the dry bone! and
with frantic shrieks, he confessed himself the
murderer.

They seized and bore him to prison; there he
related every particular of his crime, and was
executed a few weeks after at the Croix au Bailiff.

From that time the apparition ceased to haunt
the cemetery; still, as I said before, the peasants
talk mysteriously of "Revenants" hereabouts,
and do not like to linger on their way after dark.

You are now very near King's Mills, and the
first turn to the right, after passing St. George,
leads to

Vazon Bay.

This bay was formerly a forest, which the en-

croachments of the sea have swallowed up, and it
was here that an ancestor of Colonel Guille, of
St. George, discovered that the decayed wood
beneath the surface of the soil was excellent fuel,
and brought it into general use, calling it Gorban
or Corban, a gift.

It is now a most valuable article to the poor,
who assemble in parties of eight or ten to dig it
up at the spring tides. As soon as the sea ebbs
far enough, they sound with pointed iron rods
until they come to the gorban, and then clearing
the sand, in a circumference of about twelve feet,
and making drains to carry off the accumulating
water, they set to work with heavy sharp hoes,
whirling them round their heads, and cutting the
peat into great squares, which others fling out of
the pit, and the women and boys carry away in
carts, thus working hard and fast until the flow-
ing tide compels them to desist.

Birds' nests, and nuts with kernels yet sounding in them, and a few earthen vessels and pieces
of copper and stone instruments, supposed to
have been the cleavers with which the Druids
flayed their cattle, have been found here.

The lord of the " Fief le Compte," which in-
cludes the Vazon Bay, has still in his possession
deeds, by which the tenants were bound to pay a
trifling duty, called Pénage, for the privilege of
feeding their swine in the forest of the Vazon, and
that, too, in the reign of Henry II., who granted
part of the island to the Count of Mortain, from
whence the title of Fief le Compte, or Count's
Fief. This seigneur has a right to the toll of

three sous from his tenants on the marriage of
every daughter; and before the ceremony, the
bride must have leave to enter the marriage state
from the said lord or superior of the fief.

Houmet Tower,

Which juts out into the sea on the north side of
this bay, is chiefly remarkable for a cave called
" Le Creux des Fées," and the existence of a
subterraneous passage two miles long, reaching to
St. Saviour's church, which, from the confined
air and noxious vapours, it is impossible to explore.

Tradition gives a supernatural origin to this
passage, which the country people, who are still
believers in fairy-land, assert to have been the
work of some English fairies. It is said, a
country girl, passing through the Vazon *Forest*,
one morning early, perceived a great multitude of
little men, all dressed in green, hiding in the
long grass; that they were very fair and very
powerful, and suddenly starting up, they all advanced into the country, and demanded the
daughters of the land for wives, and the half of
the island for a possession. This was refused by
the Guernsey men, who did not feel disposed to
part with either; and then the little warriors
attacked them furiously, beat them all through
King's Mills, and by St. Mary's church, down to
the Amballes near the sea, and slew every living,
man and boy, except one, who lived at St. Andrew's, and hid himself in an oven. The blood
of the slain ran down like a river, at a place called

" La Rouge Rue" to this day, and the fairies
took possession of the island, and lived here many
years, when being obliged to return to their own
fairy-land, they left their wives and children behind, but returned invisibly to watch over them,
as many a dreaming girl and doting old woman
can tell. It is to this event that may be attributed
the generally small stature of Guernsey people,
and the fairness of their complexions and sylph-
like forms.

But it was also on this spot that the Sarragou-
sais, under Yvon de Galles, attacked the island
in 1372, and were discovered in like manner at
day-break by one Jean Letoc, who gave the alarm.
This time the Guernsey men, being more equally
matched against mortal foes, fought very valiantly,
and Yvon and his freebooters were chased from
the Vazon to the town, where they escaped to
their ships, and then relanded upon another
point, laying siege to St. Michael's Abbey, which
was surrendered through treachery, and Yvon
departed with much booty, exacting a tax which
is still paid, called " Les Campards."

The Village of King's Mills

Is situated in one of the most picturesque valleys,
open to the sea on one side, and sheltered by
wooded hills on the other, with three ancient
water-mills, whose proprietors in feudal times
claimed the sole prerogative of grinding corn for
their vassals, and held this privilege by the
tenure of presenting a plate of wheaten flour to

G

the court of St. Michael's, when it passed in the
procession called " La Chevauchie."

The cottages in this village are remarkable for
their extreme neatness, and the beauty of their
flower-gardens.   An orange-tree may be seen
bringing its fruit to perfection in the open air,
without more shelter in winter than a little mat-
ting.   The myrtles and roses, jessamine and
vine, cover most of the houses; and there are
some ruined ivied walls, supposed to be the remains of a monastery, on one side of the village
near the first mill.

Immediately after passing the second mill,
called " Le Moulin du Milieu," you may notice
on the right hand of the road a narrow pathway
ascending to a winding wooded walk by a brook-
side, raised many feet above the road, and leading
to the next mill—" Le Moulin du Haut." From
hence crossing the little copse beyond, you follow
the track up the hill-side, and, at its summit,
close to the windmill, there is *so* beautiful a view
of land and ocean outspread beneath you, as it is
worth turning aside to see.

In no part of the island are there more delightful walks than in this neighbourhood, the old estate of the Groignet with its ivy-gate, is nearly
opposite the " Moulin du Haut," and the continuation of this, the Talbot Road, brings you to
St. Andrew's church, through a lovely valley,
which, with its ancient water-mills, I have noticed
elsewhere.

Cobo Bay

Lies towards the Vale Parish, behind Saumarez. The Watch-tower, on the south-side, called Le Roc du Guet, has a fine view; and on the turf round it may be found the pretty lilac ixia (*trichomena bulbæcodium*), which is rare in England, and grows abundantly in this spot, flowering in April and May. There are fine loach ponds along this coast from Grande Rocque to Vazon Bay; and a rich harvest for the shell gatherer in limpets and aumer shells, which are found sticking to the rocks under the sea-weed in every little pool.

The Câtel Fair.

This is held on an open ground, between the church and a pretty little village called Le Préel. The fair takes place at Easter, Midsummer, and Michaelmas, when the display of cattle, especially cows and heifers of the insular breed, which have for many years formed a principal article of local export, may be seen to great advantage.

On these occasions the Agricultural Society distributes premiums to the proprietors of the finest and most promising heifers, as also on the finest bulls. To obtain the highest prize, it is necessary the animal should possess the 20 points which constitute perfection; it is then adorned with ribbons bearing the distinguished number, of which the proprietor is not a little proud: other prizes and ribbons are given to those who have 18 or 19 points, but not under.

The following are the different qualities necessary to a good Guernsey or Alderney cow :—

		Points.
1st.	Pedigree, as well of the bull as of the cow, yellow ears, tail, and good udder	7
2nd.	General appearance, handsome colour—cream, light red, or both mixed with white	3
3rd.	Handsome head, well horned, and bright and prominent eye	4
4th.	Deep barrel-shaped body	3
5th.	Good hind quarter and straight back	2
6th.	Handsome legs and small bones	1
	Total	20

The average price of a Guernsey cow is from
£14 to £16, but the beauty and quality of the
animal make a considerable difference in the sum.
They are known in England as Alderney cows ;
but, in point of fact, not one in twenty are from
that island ; neither are they Guernsey cows
which frequently bear the name in England, as
many of an inferior quality are exported from
Jersey ; and though it may be that the same
quantity of milk is produced by the Jersey cow,
yet it is not nearly as rich, and the butter not so
good. Real Guernsey cows are larger, taller, and
of rather a darker colour than the Jersey ones.

Les Landes du Marché.

On the borders of this parish, or rather of four
parishes, namely, The Vale, St. Sampson's, St,

Saviour's, and the Câtel, where they all meet at a spot called Les Landes du Marché, the public markets were formerly held, and it appears that a toll or duty was payable to the Crown for all goods bought here; for by a letter from Edward II., in the first year of his reign, addressed to Otho de Grandison, the governor of the island, his Majesty states: "That having been informed that the market held at the Landes had been transferred to a fief belonging to a private individual, to his prejudice, the governor was to order public proclamation to be made, that it should be held there as usual, and nowhere else." How long this command was observed we know not, but for some centuries previous to the erection of the present market, it was held in High Street, as far as the bottom of Cow Lane, so called from its being the principal meat-market. Those were the days when, every forenoon, High Street was crowded with fish vendors and vegetable baskets, to the great hindrance even of a foot passenger, and when, in summer evenings, the street being cleaned and swept, the shopkeepers sat at their own house door, gathered round small tables, at which they enjoyed their tea and gossiped with their opposite neighbours; when the noblest and wealthiest of the island seigneurs had his town-house where Bishop's shop now stands, and his *country-house* in Berthelot Street! (Peter Le Mesurier, Esq., also, then Governor of Alderney); when New Town was all rich pasture land, and the Grange Road a wild woodland; when our grandmothers walked to their club in high-heeled shoes, behind a *three-*

candled lantern, and rode on a pillion behind
our powdered grandfathers. Verily—"*Le bouan-
vier temps n'est plus !* "

St. Saviour's Parish.

This parish is situated at the western side of
the island, bounded by St. Andrew's, St. Peter's,
and the Câtel inland, and by Perelle Bay towards
the sea. The continuation of St. Andrew's Road,
after passing the small chapel belonging to the
Calvinist dissenters, branches off to the right and
left, either of which leads to

St. Saviour's Church.

This church stands upon a height, commanding a fine sea view, and looking down upon a
wooded valley sweeping round the hill. Its architecture is of the simplest Gothic style, was
built in 1154, and consecrated by the abbot of
the priory of St. Michael's, on the 30th of May,
in the presence of the noble Seigneur Walter
Dunker, then governor of the holy isle of Guernsey, the noble Martin Blundell, seneschal of the
court and abbey of St. Michael, and a full assembly of the inhabitants. The cannon in the
churchyard was formerly on

La Houque Fouque,

which is an elevation not far from the church, of
very ancient date, called La Houque Fouque, or
" Fire-Hill," from the Latin *Agger Focus,* which
was used in the early ages for a watch-place and
beacon ; when, from the frequent invasion of

pirates, it was customary upon the approach of
any considerable number of vessels to kindle fires
on this hillock, as a warning to the inhabitants,
and a signal to their friends on the French coast.
There are several of these elevations in different
directions, one called " La Houque Hatenas," at
St. Martin's; and the island of Jedthou, opposite
St. Peter's Port, most probably derives its name
from being the principal watch-tower, " Great
Houque," or Grande Houque, corrupted into
Jedthou.

Alexander's Hotel.

Not far from the church, at the bottom of the
hill, is Alexander's Hotel, celebrated for pancakes
and eggs and bacon, on the most reasonable
terms. It is a favourite place for pic-nic parties,
and steadily patronized by the students of Elizabeth College. The Union Hotel is likewise on
this road.

St. Appoline's Chapel

Is a very remarkable building, on the lower road,
which leads to King's Mills, supposed to have
been the very first chapel in the island. The
doorway and windows exhibit the Saxon arch,
the ceiling is also arched internally; there are
remains of rude fresco paintings on one of the
walls, two or three angel heads being yet visible,
and one of which is said to be a portrait of St.
Appoline; the exterior roof is angular, and covered
with small stones. This monument of antiquity
having fallen into private hands, on the distribu-
tion of monastic buildings, under Henry VIII., it
has since been made use of as a barn, and is now

filled with dried furze and other fuel, but open to
inspection, if the stranger feels interested in the
ruin.   Perhaps some further light is thrown on
this subject in Mr. Falle's History of Jersey;
who tells us, that, in the time of St. Sampson
and St. Maglorius, the first Christian mission-
aries in these islands, when the inhabitants were
converted by their preaching, they dispersed
the holy men and women of their convents, to
strengthen the faith and civilize the new con-
verts.   St. Julien and St. Jacques being their
ministers, in what is now the town, and St. Anne
and St. George having charge of St. Mary's in
the Câtel parish, it is probable that St. Appoline
dwelt amongst the fishermen at Le Rée, and
caused this little chapel to be built for their use.

The Priory of Lihou

Once stood on the small island which bears its
name, on this side of the coast.   It was erected
in 1114, and consecrated to the Virgin Mary by
the Bishop of Coûtances; but little more is known
of it, and the ground is now a rabbit warren, held
under a renewable lease from government, by
James Priaulx, Esq., who has erected a dwelling-
house beside the ruins of the priory.   In the
rocks on the south side there are two curious
natural baths, supposed to have been hollowed
out by the friction of stones washed round them
by the eddy of the strong tides in this bay.
They were most likely used by the nuns of the
convent in former times.

Fairy Footsteps.

In the bay which sweeps round the borders of
St. Peter's parish, and joins Le Reé, there is a
rock, on which is said to be the print of two human feet; and the account given by a fisherman,
who was questioned on the subject, attributes the
foot marks to the Lady of Lihou, a prioress of the
convent. He said that, once upon a time, on the
opposite point of Pleinmont, there lived a very
holy man, in great retirement, conversing with
none, and never leaving his cell, except to administer the sacraments and consolations of religion.
No person ever ventured to visit him, and he was
seen to kneel for hours before the cross which
stood upon the cliff. But one night a fisherman,
who had moored his boat close in shore, and was
watching the tide, intending to drift off with it
for early fishing, saw by the moon's light, about
the midnight hour, this holy hermit cross the
sands, and meet a small slight figure, wrapped in
a mantle, which came from the direction of the
priory. They stood together on this rock for
what seemed to him a long time, and then they
parted, each returning the way they came; and
the thing seemed so incredible, that when morning dawned the fisherman thought he had but
dreamt of the occurrence. However, curiosity
led him to examine the place; and what was his
surprise at finding on the hard rock the print of
two little feet. He related what he had seen on
the preceding night, but was scarcely believed,

until it was discovered that the hermit's cell was
forsaken, and he was never more seen or heard of.

Le Creux des Fées.

There is another haunted cave on one side of
this bay, called " Le Creux des Fées, dangerous
to walk in after night-fall, by reason of the fairy
folks who dwell there.

Vraicing.

All round this coast from Lihou to Cobo Bay,
the marine herb or algæ, called vraic, is very
plentiful. This sea-weed, which is used both as
fuel and manure, is of the greatest value to the
farmers, and of the utmost importance to the
poor fishermen, who being unable to afford coal
or wood for the winter, depend upon this for
firing, and sell the ashes for manure; about
twenty bushels are requisite for one vergée of land.

There are two kinds of vraic, the "vraic scié,"
so called from being cut from the rock with a
small reaping-hook, and the " vraic venant,"
being washed on the coast and gathered after
every spring-tide, particularly if the weather is
stormy. So important is this article in the island,
that certain restrictions specified in the ordinances of the court are laid upon the time and
manner of its appropriation.

Poor persons who possess neither horse nor
cart are allowed to cut it during the first eight
days of the first spring-tide after Easter, provided
they carry it on their backs to the beach.

The manner of cutting and gathering this product is worth noticing. On the morning of the appointed days hundreds of country people assemble from all parts, two or three families joining company, some with carts, and some with horses, having panniers slung on each side of them; they proceed to the beach, and as the tide ebbs they scatter themselves over the bays, the most active, on foot or on horseback, wading to the rocks, as far out as possible. Some going in boats to detached rocks, even at a great distance, and being all armed with small bill-hooks, they cut away as fast as possible, sending it off in boat-loads to the beach, where it is deposited in heaps, upon which a smooth stone is laid, having the initials of the owner chalked upon it.

The scene is such a merry one that the stranger will be repaid for a walk or ride to either of these bays on a vraicing day : the odd costumes of both men and women, with trousers and petticoats tucked up for greater freedom of limb; the varied dress of the younger ones, who turn out on this occasion with as much delight as on a holiday; those who cannot cut vraic being employed in carrying it; whilst most of the women gather *aumers*, crabs, and limpets in such prodigious quantities that the market is always overstocked with them on these occasions. It is most amusing to watch these vraicers—the gallantry of the young farmers, who pause in their labour to assist some favourite maiden in turning over a large stone, under which she is *sure* that there *must* be a quantity of aumers—the scrambling in shallow

pools for some unlucky crab, who has incautiously
left his hiding place—the many falls over the slip-
pery sea-weed, and the peals of laughter which
resound on all sides.   Here a group of merry children with their broken knives hitting off the limpets (called in their Guernsey dialect "des flies"),
and filling the basket slung across their shoulders,
each one trying to collect the greatest number,
and every now and then tempted to give chase to
a fine loach or cabot, which darts across the pond
in utter dismay at the commotion in his quiet
home.   There a still noisier group of *grown-up
children*, hindering one another with rustic co-
quetry, and called to order by some gruff voice in
the distance, which sets them all at work again in
a minute.

At the close of the day, when the tide has
risen to its height, and the retreating labourers are
fairly beaten back to the sandy beach, the younger
ones conclude the business by a general bathing;
and a whole string of twenty or more, men and
woman alternately, each securing the hand he
loves best, march into the water as far they can,
and duck each other heartily; splashing, tum-
bling, screaming, laughing, and then go home
thoroughly soaked, but as light-hearted as they
are heavy-footed, to enjoy a plentiful supper of
shell-fish, fried aumers and boiled limpets, which
are very excellent eating for those who have good
digestions.

The " vraic venant" is not gathered in the same
manner; it is mostly done in rough weather, when
the boisterous waves having torn it from the rocks,

it is cast upon the beach, and the men send out
immense rakes, with which they drag the vraic
on shore, beyond the reach of the sea.   This employment is the most laborious, from the weight
and strain of the heavy rakes; and not without
some danger, as they are often wrenched from
their hands, and brought violently back against
the legs of the men, who thus risk broken limbs,
as the shingles dragged by the tide from beneath
their feet cause many tumbles and drenchings.

It has been ascertained that nearly 24,000 loads
of *vraic venant*, each worth two shillings, when
taken at the beach; and about 1200 loads of
vraic scié, each worth twelve shillings, are yearly
collected on this coast, the value of which may be
stated in round numbers at about £3000 sterling.

Marine Plants.

This vraic is the only manure used in the
island, except at St. Sampson's, where they import chalk for the low marshy grounds.

Both in Alderney, and on some parts of this
coast, a sea-weed is collected, which is equal in
virtue to the celebrated Icelandic moss, and used
in the same manner for invalids.   The Algæ of
Serk afford a substitute for horse-hair of the
finest quality.

There are abundance of corals, corallines, and
curious marine plants, in all these bays; but the
stranger will do well to take a boy-guide with
him on these expeditions, or to keep a sharp look-
out after the tide, which is very rapid and

H

treacherous, sweeping round the rocks in all directions.

Antiquities at St. Saviour's.

There is a small Druidical altar at Le Rée, and another at the extremity of the rocky bridge forming the south-west headland of Perelle Bay, between Le Rée and Richmond barracks. This spot is called the Cackieuro, which some suppose to be a corruption of *Catel au Roc*, Castle on a Rock, but no traces of a building are discernible; and it is chiefly remarkable in Guernsey demonology as the trysting-place of all the native witches and evil spirits who meet here for the purpose of accounting to their master, the archfiend, and worshipping him. At the Record Office may be seen many confessions made by reputed sorcières, or witches, who were condemned to be burnt alive for their wickedness; and though these accusations are no longer tolerated by the court, yet the existence and actual practice of witchcraft are still devoutly believed by the peasants; as also the reality of fairies. If the visitor can speak Guernsey French, he may hear some curious stories from the people hereabouts.

A tomb was discovered in this parish in 1818, by some planters, on the farm of Mr. Thomas Lainé; the grave was six feet nine inches in length, walled on each side; at the bottom, on the left side, were found a sabre in a steel scabbard, a pike lance, with a handle of cedar-wood, and a small brass ornament. This was supposed to have been the tomb of a war-chief, perhaps of a Roman.

A vase was discovered in the same field some days after, full of black clayish earth; and on several stones some illegible inscriptions; all of which are in the possession of Mr. Lainé, who is kind enough to shew them to the curious.

A purse of leather, containing about 700 coins, the greater part silver pennies, and the rest copper, were found, in 1829, in a field at Rocquaine, called Le Catillon. The coins were of the reigns of Philip, King of France, and Edward the Second of England.

There are three dissenting chapels in this parish, Methodist, Calvinist, and Baptist, with a Sunday school attached to each.

The present curate of this parish is the Rev. Peter Carey.

CHAPTER IV.

THE PARISH OF ST. PETER'S-IN-THE-WOOD.

St. Peter-in-the-Wood is bounded by St. Saviour's, the Forest, the Torteval, and Le Rée.

The Church

Is one of the neatest and most picturesque in the island; a plain gothic building, supported by buttresses, tastefully arranged; and its tower, with castellated parapet, has a good effect, particularly from the lower part of the road winding to the sea and Rocquaine Bay. This church was con-

secrated by Bartholomew Bassel, Bishop of Coûtance, the 29th of June, 1167, and once stood in
the midst of forest land, of which no trace
remains.

The only object of peculiar interest in this
parish is a monument of antiquity, a

Cromlech,

situated about half a mile from the church, on
the Le Rée road, supposed to be one of the most
perfect in the island. It consists of a large block
of granite, placed erect, in height about ten feet,
in width about three. History throws no light
upon this altar, but tradition, of course, has invested it with fictitious interest. Asking a coun-
tryman once—"Have you heard how that stone
came there?" The answer was: "*Mais vére—
jai oui dire à des vielles gens que t'ché du temps
des faès, et que t'ché une petite femme qui l'porti
là dans son devanti—èpi d'autres disent que t'ché
là que les petits gens jouai aux pllates et picqui-
rent chette roc pour la merque assai.*" The
English of which is, that he had heard from the
old people, that in the time when the fairies were
occasionally seen, a "Little Ladye" carried this
great stone from the sea up to this spot! Others
assert that, when the fairies played at skittles,
they set up this stone as a mark! We cannot
exactly decide the point at present.

There are several good schools in this parish,
and the present Rector is the Rev. Thomas
Brock, Surrogate to the Dean.

Torteval Parish.

The parish of Torteval joins that of St. Peter's and the Forest.

The Church,

Which is dedicated to St. Philip, was consecrated on the 1st day of November, 1130. It is said to have been built by one Philip de Carteret, a native of Jersey, who, encountering a dreadful storm at sea, made a vow that, if Providence should spare his life, he would build a church on the first land to which he came. The vessel miraculously made the harbour in Rocquaine Bay, about midnight, on the 13th day of September, 1129, and he accordingly performed his vow by erecting the church, which, having fallen into decay, was replaced by the present building some few years ago.

From an eminence not far from the church, towards Pleinmont Point, a very fine view is obtained of Rocquaine Bay, and all the precipitous, rocky coast on this side of the island. In stormy weather, particularly when the wind is blowing hard from the south-west, the scene is awfully grand; nothing can exceed the violence with which the rude waves rush towards the shore, springing over the Hanois Rock, in sheets of silvery spray, with the noise of thunder. This dangerous ridge extends nearly two miles off the land, and many a noble ship has been wrecked amongst its breakers; amongst others, H. M. ship Boreas was lost in November, 1808, not many hours after leaving St. Peter's Port in fine weather, and but few of her crew were saved. In 1835, a great part of this wreck was brought up by means of a diving apparatus, under the direction of the Guernsey Sub-Marine Company. The Hanois Rocks once joined the shore, as may be ascertained from the remains of a gateway on one of them, and the track of a cart-road still visible at low tide. They were probably separated from the island at the time when the forest of Vazon Bay was overflowed.

The Creux Mahie.

The Creux Mahie or Malier, on the south side of this parish, is a natural cavern, about 200 feet in length and 40 or 50 feet wide, rising from 20 to 60 feet in height, broken and uneven at the bottom, with an irregular vaulted roof.

Whether this is an excavation made by the sea, or of volcanic origin, has not been decided; the roof exhibits many stalactical formations, an appearance very unusual in the absence of lime, which has been found in no part of the island.

The descent to this cave is not at all difficult; but the stranger will require a guide, (which any child from the neighbouring cottages will be,) as the entrance to this cave is so small as to be imperceptible until actually beside it, and then it looks scarcely large enough to pass through. Lights must be taken to explore it; or a bundle of furze is best, which being divided here and there, and fires lighted at different points, the whole cavern will be illuminated, and the effect is wild and beautiful.

This parish with the Forest forms one rectory at present, held by the Rev. Daniel Dobree; there are an endowed school, a Sunday school, and dissenting chapels with their schools.

The Forest.

All that this parish can boast of is the scenery of Petit Bo Bay and Moyer Point.

The Church

Is a Gothic building, the roof of which seems to have been originally small stones, imbedded in mortar; but recent repairs have nearly tiled it. It was consecrated on the 3rd of September, 1163, by Silvestre de Brunievre, Bishop of Coûtance, and dedicated to St. Margaret; the curate himself placed the gilded cock on the pinnacle. There is nothing here to detain the stranger from a delightful walk to

Moyer Point,

from whence he has a beautiful view of the bold coast, passing through a ravine, with two fishermen's huts on one side, and the mingled heath and furze, soft turf and wild flowers clasping the rude rocks, round the sweeping hill, from whose pathway, at the turn of the road, a magnificent expanse of ocean is beheld. A sheltered cave at the extremity of this track gives anchorage to a group of fishing-boats, which may be hired, if the stranger would enjoy a sail to Petit Bo or Saint's Bay; or if he is an amateur of fishing, there are abundance of rock-fish, whitings, sword-fish, &c., immediately off this Point.

The road between the Forest and St. Martin's is singularly uninteresting, though fertile and well cultivated; but from it there is a road branching off to

Petit Bo Bay,

one of the most beautiful in the island, and a favourite resort with pic-nic parties. The approach to it is through a deep ravine, with a streamlet, on the borders of which wild flowers grow in profusion, affording a rich harvest to the botanist, as he may there find many plants accounted rare in England. A water-mill, half concealed by a group of elms, stands within a few paces of the martello tower at the entrance of the bay, and a farmhouse where refreshment may be obtained; the Guernsey buttermilk and eggs and bacon, or if desired, doubtless, the real Guernsey "*soupe à la graisse;*" this latter, however delicious it is deemed by the natives, is hardly to the taste of an English palate; it consists of a quantity of cabbage boiled in water, with a spoonful of grease or piece of rancid bacon, and thickened slightly with flour and water; nevertheless it is the daily food of the peasants, who very rarely taste butcher's meat, and when living in town, where good beef and mutton are provided from their master's table, are frequently known to pine for their "soupe à la graisse," and make it for themselves as a great treat.

CHAPTER V.

ST. MARTIN'S PARISH

Joins that of the Town and St. Andrew's. The road from town to St. Martin's is by the Grange and Petite Marche; at Colbourne Place, turn to the right, and then it is optional whether you take the first turning after that on the left, which will lead you to the church; or walk on by Ross Place and continue in the St. Andrew's Road, passing Havilland Hall, the seat of Colonel de Havilland, at present the residence of the Lieut.-Governor General Napier. When you reach the top of the hill you find yourself at the Croix au Bailiff, and whilst the road runs directly on to St. Andrew's and St. Peter's-in-the-Wood, by turning to the left you will soon reach

St. Martin's Church,

a low Gothic building, with a tower, pinnacles, and lofty spire, the interior presenting a few ancient monuments; it was consecrated by Bersabel le Blanc, Bishop of Coûtance, in February, 1199, in the presence of the Governors of Rennes, Honfleur, Caen, Totnes, Southampton, and upwards of eighty-four feudal lords, each displaying his banner. It must have been an imposing sight, and interesting to see so many haughty warriors engaged in the solemn rite of dedicating the newbuilt temple to their God, and offering largely (which they all did) of their substance towards its treasury, though very few of these contributors had any personal interest in this church, being natives of England and France.

The present rector is the Rev. R. Potenger.

The manor-house of Sausmarez is in this parish, an ancient building on the road from St. Peter's Port, with armorial supporters over the gateway: the manor has been a fief in the De Sausmarez family nearly three hundred years. There are several rooms hung with tapestry, the subjects from Ovid's Metamorphoses, and the collection of family paintings is extensive. The pleasant shady lane opposite, which passes by Bonair, leads to

Doyle's Monument.

This is a plain round column of granite, ninety-six feet in height from the base, and about four hundred feet from the level of the sea, with a winding staircase in the interior, reaching to the top, on which is a projecting square gallery secured with railings; the key of this tower is kept at a neighbouring house, and the view from the summit is well worth the ascent.

It was erected by the Guernsey States, in grateful remembrance of many public services rendered to the Island, by the late General Sir John Doyle, whilst Lieutenant-Governor of the Island, from 1803 to 1817.

The Promontory of Jerbourg,

On which are Jerbourg barracks, is immediately below the column; it was on this spot that Robert of Normandy raised a castle for the defence and protection of the inhabitants, at the same time that "Le Château des Marais," Ivy Castle, was built, but not a vestige of this remains. The office of castellan, or keeper of the castle, was held by the De Saumarez family. Tradition asserts that this castle was erected on the ruins of a Roman fortification, and several parallel ditches may be traced round it which give probability to the conjecture.

The walk round this point to

Moulin Huet

is more beautiful than pen can describe. There is a lane leading to the cliff almost overgrown with waving fern and hanging woodbine; the briar-rose, the forget-me-not, veronica, the blue bell, with a hundred other sweet wild flowers, thronging the hedges on either side, and the turf at our feet. The warbling of the thrush mingles with the cry of the sea-bird, and the murmur of the wild-bee with the music of the waters below— the lights and shadows, from the broken precipitous rocks, fall on the shingly and sandy beach, where cool, quiet resting-places are offered by the dark caves; and where in hidden nooks fine deep loach ponds, and shallow pools, offer sport both to the fisher and the shell gatherer. The estate of the Vallon belonging to De Vic Carey, Esq., opens upon this delightful bay, and yet is protected from the sea-breeze by a well-wooded shrubbery. In the valley on the opposite side are a paper-manufactory and water-mill; and round the extreme point the pretty harbour-age of

Saints Bay

is discovered, where formerly an archbishop of
Rouen, uncle to William the Conqueror, took
refuge when banished from his native country.
There are some very ancient farm-houses in this
neighbourhood, tenanted by families bearing the
archbishop's name, Manger, and said to be his
descendants. No remains of his hermitage can
be traced.

This is a very fertile parish, with many good
dwelling-houses and lodgings, the air being pecu-
liarly bracing and salubrious; invalids are generally recommended to try it. The only point
that remains to be noticed is

Fermain Bay;

which, being within an easy walk of the town,
and a quiet, pleasant spot, is deservedly a great
favourite. The road to it winds through a well-
watered valley, verdant at all seasons of the year;
and a gurgling stream falls into the sea, through
the shingle on the beach, which has some very
fine pebbles, agates, and jaspers, amongst the
sand at low water. It is defended by a martello
tower and battery. The white tower on the cliff
to the left is a landmark, placed there for the
purpose of pointing out to mariners coming down
the Great Russel, the situation of a dangerous
cluster of rocks, about half way between this
point and the centre of Sark, called the Lower
Heads.

Taking the narrow track to the right, and following it along the cliff to the south-west point, brings the stranger to a bold rock, called Arthur's Seat, which juts out towards the sea, and gives a fine view of Fort George, the islands of Serk, Herm, and Jedthou, with the little harbour of Bec du Nez, a famous fishing station on the right, and a whole line of coast. A pleasant spot indeed it is for a quiet resting-place; where both the painter's eye, and the poet's heart, may be gladdened by the beauty of earth, sea, and sky.

St. Andrew's Parish

Is the only one in the island which does not in some part border on the sea.

The Church

Is about two miles from town, a plain, low Gothic building, supported by buttresses, with a castellated tower at the west; it was consecrated by the abbot of St. Michael, under the authority of the Bishop of Coûtance, on the first day of October, 1224. It is prettily situated in a valley, and the sheltered churchyard boasts of the earliest violets in the island. The parsonage-house is quite close to it. The rectors of this parish have long held a field for the service of performing mass, when the seigneur of the fief, St. Helena, holds his court; but since the Reformation the Lord's Prayer has been substituted for the mass. The Rev. William Guille is the present rector. On the road from the church of St. Peter's to St. Saviour's, but not far from it, is the manor-house of St. Helena, the residence of John Carey, Esq.;

I

and, some way beyond that, the estate of the
Vaubellets, belonging to Frederick Mansell, Esq.
The road here winds through a sheltered part of
the country; and one of the lanes to the right
leads to the village called

Le Hurel,

a collection of mere huts; rude, dirty-looking cottages, but remarkable from the people who tenant
it.   They are a kind of half-gipsy, half-beggar
race, bearing the name of Pipet; and kept totally
distinct from every other family, because no person would intermarry with them upon any consideration.   Their appearance and features are
quite unlike the rest of the Guernsey peasantry,
who are extremely good-looking, clean, and active; whereas these Pipets may be found basking
in the sun, with anything but a prepossessing
exterior.   The country people consider them as
wizards and witches; and at certain times of the
year, about Christmas, when they are privileged
to go round and beg for their *Noël*, or "*irvières*,"
new years' gifts, no one likes to send them away
empty-handed, for fear of the consequences to
themselves, their cattle, or their children.

Le Moulin de l'Echelle.

The stranger is strongly recommended to walk
from St. Andrew's Church to King's Mills, by
the Talbot Road; it is certainly the most picturesque in the island,—the farm-houses so neat
and cheerful, the cottages so bright-looking, with
their mantles of myrtles and roses, and the hedges

so fragrant with the flowering furze. There are coppices on the left, through which a streamlet runs for some miles, turning in its course some ancient water-mills, the first of which is called Le Moulin de l'Echelle, from the circumstance that, formerly, the miller was bound to the service of taking care of the ladder used at executions; which took place in this parish at the first cross roads from town, on the upper road to the Câtel parish.

Le Croix au Bailiff.

This spot is called Le Croix au Bailiff from the following circumstance :—

At the commencement of the thirteenth century, the Bailiff of the island was one Gaultier de la Salle, who lived about half-a-mile from this place, at the Ville au Roi, which still may be seen with its sculptured granite door-way, and a granite spiral staircase, tenanted only by poor people, and surrounded with out-houses, yet preserving the dignity of its age by ivy-mantled walls, and the venerable trees which hang over it. This Gaultier de la Salle had a poor neighbour, named Massey, who chiefly depended for support on the produce of a small patch of ground joining the Bailiff's estate, through which he had the right of passage to a well belonging to La Salle.

This privilege was a great annoyance to the gentleman, and he tried various means to deprive the poor man of it; but being unsuccessful in them all, he formed a wicked plan for taking away his life.

In those days theft was often a capital crime,—in some cases invariably so,— and La Salle, hiding two of his own silver cups, and expressing very strong suspicions of his neighbour, Massey was taken up and brought to trial.   His accuser being a person of such high authority, who was supported besides by corrupted witnesses, the case was soon made clear to the judges; they unanimously found poor Massey "guilty," and came forth from the last deliberation with the sentence of death upon their lips.

There was a pause—a dead silence in the court; and the unfortunate prisoner, after vainly asserting his innocence, awaited his condemnation hopelessly; when suddenly a noise was heard, the trampling of many feet, and a man rushed breathlessly into the court, holding up the silver cups, and exclaiming, "They are found;" he informed the judges that, having been employed that morning in removing some sheaves of corn into the barn, he and his fellow-labourers had found the cups in the middle of the rick.   Hardly had he said this, than De la Salle passionately exclaimed, "Fool—did I not tell thee *not* to touch *that* rick; I knew ——." He stopped in confusion, but his words were marked.   Every eye was turned on the guilty Bailiff, and the court resolved that the base accuser should suffer the *lex talionis*, or punishment which he had contrived for his victim.   Massey was instantly set at liberty; and, after a short trial, Gaultier de la Salle was sentenced to death. On his way to execution, he stopped at this spot and partook of the sacrament, in remembrance of which a cross was erected, called "The Bailiff's Cross."

The spot is now only marked by a stone in the pathway, with a cross marked upon it. The place where Massey lived is called "Le Courtil Massey," or Massey's Field, to this day.

The Croix au Bailiff Road.

The continuation of this road leads directly to the Câtel Church, and branches off to the right down to the picturesque valley of the

Foulon;

or to the left, farther on, through some beautiful lanes, which wind over hill and dale, passing by Woodlands to King's Mills, and here and there opening upon delightful views, the sea on one side, and the richly cultivated country on the other.

CHAPTER VI.

GUERNSEY SUPERSTITIONS.

GUERNSEY has had its superstitions; it has them even *now* in this age of common sense; even now when the light of Christianity has chased away the gross darkness of other days, and makes it a marvel that any such can find a hiding-place in the land. The superstitions of old no where more stoutly flourished than in these little islands, and I would bewail and bitterly condemn the absurd fragments of some of them which remain, had I

I 3

not first learnt the fairy lore of Guernsey, and first heard tales of "Diablérie" and "Sorcellérie," by the nursery fire, and at the cottage hearth.

Often have I listened to "Les Vielles Histoires" until my young heart quaked with horror, and my hurried steps homeward, and quick glances from side to side, told how nearly I was starting at every mis-shapen bush for a "sorcier" or shrinking from my own shadow as a "revenant." The fairy tales indeed are pretty and innocent enough. (See page 48 for the history of the English fairies, who came over and took possession of the island at the time when Vazon Bay was an extensive forest.) The legend of the "Creux des Fèes" at Houmêt Tower seems to have the same foundation as a common fairy tale in England and Scotland. The Guernsey version of "The Fairy Child" is as follows :—

L' Histoire du p'tit Colinet.

A great many years ago, in the time when fairy-folk used often to appear, and sometimes talk to people, a good woman named Lizabeau, who lived at King's Mills, was roused out of her midnight sleep by a great knocking at her door, and a man's voice bidding her get up quickly, for she was wanted. Lizabeau was a widow who often attended her neighbours as a sick or lying-in-nurse, and therefore was neither surprised nor frightened, but dressed quickly and opened her door. The man was of very small stature, wrapped in a cloak, and as she advanced a light, he turned aside saying, she was wanted to see a sick child. The good woman had never seen him before, and hesitated, but he set off walking very fast, and she presently followed him up the road and saw him turn down towards Vazon Bay. That was strange, for only fishermen lived there, and as her guide looked like a gentleman, though he was so *very small,* she expected to be led towards town, or St. George; and after walking a few steps beside him, she said,

"Sir, you must have taken the wrong road, this leads to the sea."

"I am quite right," he replied, "*follow me.*"

And they went on. By and by they came upon the sandy shore, and Lizabeau spoke again,

"There are no houses hereabouts, sir, you have certainly lost your way. If you would tell me where you live"—

She felt dreadfully frightened, but he answered in a sweet soft voice,

"You shall see presently, good woman, *follow me.*" And they went on again. At last they crossed the sands, and came to the rocks by Houmêt Tower; it was very dark, and she could hardly find her footing; there she stopped and said, "I cannot go any further, we shall fall into the sea."

"Give me your hand," said the strange little man. She did so, and his hand was soft and small as a child's, yet leading her on so boldly, and carefully, that her fear went away, and she only wondered where she was going to. They had entered a cave, and she could not see a step before her; still they walked on and on in the total darkness,

until the man desired her to stop, and asked her
" if she did not see any thing."   *   •   •
•   •   •   •   •   •   •

Lizabeau never told what she saw, but the next
day she had a weakly little baby in her arms,
and all she answered to the many questions about
him was, " A gentleman gave him to me." The
neighbours talked a great deal, and marvelled
greatly whose child it might be, but they were
tired of talking at last, and by the time that little
Colin was seven years old, it was almost forgotten
that he was not Lizabeau's child.

He was a very beautiful boy, with wild spark-
ling eyes, and long fair hair, but *so small*, that
many of the peasant children at-three years old
were as tall as he, and much stouter; however,
he was altogether unlike other children, he never
played with them, or went to school, or did any
thing but wander about by the sea-side, sometimes bringing home fish, sometimes only shells
and sea-weed, but often telling his "mother Lizabeau," as he called her, of a strange man dressed
in green, who used to watch him in his solitary
play, and sometimes watch him *in his sleep* too.
Lizabeau did not like to hear him speak so at all,
she bid him be silent; and as Colin grew older,
he never told her of these things, for he saw that
they vexed her, and he loved his kind nurse very
dearly.

When Colin was about fifteen years old, the
minister of the parish reproved Lizabeau for never
having sent him to school, and for not making
the boy work. Lizabeau did not know well what

to say, not wishing to tell how wild and wilful
he was; but somehow the boy's bright eyes won
the good minister's heart, and he asked Colin if
he would come and work for him. Colin had
lived about twelve months with his new friend,
behaving as wisely and steadily as possible, when
it happened one night that his master came home
late from St. Saviour's Parish, and passing by a
large stone, called Le Roc du Coq chant, a voice
was heard to cry, "*Jean du Maresq—Jean du
Maresq, dites donc au petit Colin que le Grand
Colin est mort.*"

The minister was astonished, and frightened;
and as soon as he came home, he called the boy,
and said, " Colin, I heard a voice to-night saying
to me '*Dites donc au petit Colin que le grand Colin
est mort.*' "

" Ah!" exclaimed the boy hastily, "then farewell, master, I must be gone."

" Go! where?" said his master.

"I cannot tell you," replied Colinet, "farewell,
do not detain me."

" Well, but I owe you wages," said the minister, "stay till I pay them to you."

The boy laughed. " Never mind that," said
he, "there is no lack of silver or gold where I
am going," and rushing out of the door, he disappeared in the darkness of the night, leaving the
good minister in great perplexity.

That same night Lizabeau woke up to find her
foster-child standing by her bedside weeping. She
started, and said, " Colinet, my son, what ails
you ?"

" Because," said he, " because I am going a far
journey, and I may never see my earthly mother
again; and because I know that, in the land where
I am going, silver and gold will never buy me
such love as thine. Bless me, my dear mother,
bless me, for I *must* go."

Then very quickly, and before she could think
what to answer, he vanished away. Lizabeau
thought it was a dream, and the next morning
rose early, went to the minister's house, and
sought for her dear boy—he was not there—he
was never seen again; and his foster-mother pined
away for a few months, then on her death-bed
told how he was given to her, and told more than
I have related, because the story is already
too long for this little book. I must only refer
you to what I have said elsewhere about fairy
footsteps, and the little ladye who carried the
great stone at St. Peter's up from the sea-side in
her apron!

All these stories are more than half believed
even now by the country people; not three years
ago, I was riding on the beach at Rocquaine, and
stopped a fisherman to ask if he could shew me
the Fairy Cave; and in conversing, I inquired if
he had ever seen any of the fairy folk. " No," he
replied very gravely, " but my grandfather did;"
and then he told me a *very true* story, which
I do not remember well enough to repeat it.

These are innocent superstitions, such as are
found in every country, varying with the manners and customs of the different people, and I do
not know if we have gained much by the banish-

ment of these beautiful unseen from our woods and rocky shores. I do not even know that we thereby prove our wisdom, or advance nearer the truth, for

"Millions of spiritual creatures walk the earth,
"Unseen, both when we wake, and when we sleep."

Witchcraft.

But I must turn now to a darker page—the annals of witchcraft in Guernsey. Even at the present time there are wretched old women pointed at, and shunned as sorcières (I could name several were it wise or prudent), after whom servants and farmers' wives slyly throw a pinch of salt, or an old shoe, to cross the ill luck she may have left behind her. Moreover I remember terrible spells performed in our kitchen about eighteen years ago, to punish an old fish-woman who was believed to have bewitched not only the butter, the meat, and the cattle, but the child who could never thrive, they said, unless it was desorcellai ! !

It is a melancholy fact that many persons, both men and women, were tortured and burnt for this supposed crime as late as the seventeenth century. I am indebted to Mr. Burroughes, the baptist minister, for a copy of some of the trials and confessions of sorcières, before the royal court in 1617, when Amice de Carterette presided as bailiff.

Three unfortunate women, by name Collecte du Mont, Veuve Jean Bicquet, Mariè sa Fille, femme de Pierre Massi, et Isabel Bicquet femme

de Jean le Moigne, were then accused and *fully
convicted* of sorcellirie, condemned to be " pendues,
etranglées, osciès, et brulées, jusqu'à ce que leur
chair et oisements soient réduis en cendres, et
leur cendres espacées." After which sentence
they were cruelly put to the question, and a
horrid confession extorted from each of them. I
shall transcribe *part* of Collecte Bicquet's confession, some of the details being unfit for publication ; and I shall not attempt a translation !

Confession du Collecte du Mont.

" La dite question lui etant appliqué, a con-
fessés quelle était encore jeune lorsque le diable
en forme d'un chat s'apparut à elle en la paroisse
de Torteval lorsqu'elle retournait de son bétail
étant encore jour, et qu'il prit occasion de la
séduire pour l'invité à se venger de ses voisins
avec les quelles elle etait pour lors en querelle
pour quelque dommages qu'elles avait récus par la
bêtes de ceux, que dépuis quelle avait eu querelle
avec quelqu'un, il se representait à elle en la sus-
dite forme, et quelque fois en forme de chien,
l'induissant à se venger de ceux contre lesquelles
elle etait fachée, la persuadant de faire mourrir
personnes et bétes. Que le diable l'etant venue
querir pour aller au Sabbat l'appellit sans qu'on
s'appercut, et lui donnait un certain argent noir
duquel après s'étre depouillée et frotteé le dos, le
ventre, et l'estomac, et s'etant revétue sortait sans
bruit, lorsqu'elle était incontinent emportée par
l'air d'une grande vitesse. Elle se trouvait a
l'instant au lieu du Sabbat qui etait parfois au

cimetierè de la Paroisse et quelquefois proche le
rivage de la mer proche le chateau de Rocquaine, ou étant arrivé s'y rencontraient souvent
15 ou 16 sorciers et sorcières avec les diables
qui etaient là en forme de chiens, chats, et lièvres.

Lesquelles sorciers et sorcières n'a pu recon-
naitre parcequ'ils etaient tous noirs et défigurées,
bien il est vrai que le diable les enseignait par
leurs noms et le nommant, et se souvient entre
autres de la femme Calaise, et de la Hardie. A
confessé qu'a l'entrée du Sabbat les voulant
évoquer commençaient par elle—quelquefois par
Mariè sa fille condamné pour pareil crime, et
quelle l'amenat par deux fois au Sabbat avec elle
ne sachant par où le Diable l'emenait. Qu'au
Sabbat après avoir adoré le diable   *   *
*   *   *   *   *   *   *   *   *
ils buvaient du vin, ne scait de quelle couleur
que le diable versait hors d'un pot dans un gobelet
d'argent, ou d'etain, lequel vin lui semblait
comme celui qu'on boit ordinairement, et man-
geait aussi du pain blanc qui leur presentait, mais
n'a jamais vue de sel au Sabbat. Elle a confessé,
que le diable lui avait chargeé d'appeler en pas-
sant, Isabel le Moigne, et que le diable lui
contait plusieurs maux, et pour effet lui donna
certaines poudres noires qui lui commandait
de jeter sur les personnes qu'elle voudrait. Se
souvient entre autres avoir jetté sur Mons. Dollief
le ministre de sa paroisse et lui cosà la mort;
par cette même poudre; encore là, la femme de
Jean Marquis la fit mourrir par son sort quelle
touchà par son côté; et jetta de cette poudre sur

K

la femme de Mons. Perchand successor du dit
Mons. Dollief etant pour lors enceinte, et la fit
mourrir elle et son fruit. Que sur le réfus que
la femme de Thomas Tosdevin lui fit de lui
donnée du lait, lui fit assecher sa vâche en
jettant sur icelle de cette poudre, laquelle vache
elle a guerie après en lui faisant manger du son,
et de l'herbe terrestre."

The other women under the wringing of the
rack, confessed similar delusions and crimes, ac-
cusing at the same time other persons as accom-
plices. They were executed; and the record
mentions also the following sentences against
witchcraft about the same year :—

August 18, 1617.—Jeanne Guignon, femme de
    Jos. le Gallais—a été brulée toute en vie.

August 20, 1617.—Michelle veuve, Jaqueline Salmon et Anne Massisa fille—pendues et brulées.

October 17, 1617.—Phillipe veuve, Jean Nicolle
    bruleè toute en vie.

May 8, 1622.—Collette l'Etat veuve, Thomas
Tourgis et Collette Robin—pendues et brulées.

October 17, 1622.—Thomas Tourgis de la Foret,
    Jeanne Tourgis sa fille, et Michelle Syrvet,
    femme Pierre Emont—condamnés a etre brulés
    toute en vie, et leurs os reduis en cendres.

Collected Le Pelley, Esther Henri, Jeanne
Berlsam, Thomas Syrvet, Roland Henri, Mar-
guerite Picol, Jacqueline Salmon, Thomas
Heaume, Mariè Guilbert, Elizabeth Sauvrain,
David de la Mare ;—tous brulés et pendus.

Diablerie,

Or bodily appearances of the Evil One, is a firmly accredited opinion, and the foundation of innumerable stories. I will relate one as a specimen, but it loses immensely to me in its translation from the dear old Guernsey French, in which I learnt it; besides, the confidential tone which whispered it one night over the fitful blaze of a buquet or a faggot fire, gave a glow and a *truth* to the tale, which my English version sadly fails in.

A poor country girl was one day working in the fields with some young companions who were talking with great delight of the next day's holiday, and how they intended going to "*es mourtes*" and "*au son*,"* who they should see, what they should wear, &c.; and this girl was equally anxious to join the party, but she had a hard master and mistress who made her work early and late, and she was afraid to ask leave for a whole holiday. However she did ask, and was refused *en la rouannant*, which means rated her soundly for her idleness. Her master sent her to work the next morning at day-break, and marked her a double task to do before *mèjour*. She was very sorrowful, and more so when about eight o'clock several of her acquaintances passed by in their militia dress, and shouted to her to make haste and come. She began to cry, and ex-

* *Es mourtes*, the militia review; *au son*, the country dances.

claimed aloud, " Oh, what would I give for this
one holiday ! Oh, I wish somebody would help me
with my work." Presently, up came a gentleman
all in black, and asked her what she was crying
for.   She told him the cause : he replied, " Well,
if you will give me the first knot you tie to-morrow morning, I'll get your work done, and you
shall go."   Quite overjoyed, the poor girl agreed.
Immediately the weeds were pulled up by invisible hands, gathered in bundles very neatly, and
more than her task accomplished in an hour.
She had plenty of time now to get to L'Hyvreuse
before the firing began, and hurried off to her
master, who was surprised at her unusual diligence, and let her go.   All day long she was
happy enough, but when she went to the evening
" son " her heart grew heavier and heavier as she
remembered her promise to the dark gentleman :
she could not dance, she was so uneasy, and when
night came on she was more and more frightened.   At last she could bear it no longer, and
went to the minister of the parish, to whom with
many tears she told all that had passed.   He bade
her not to be afraid, but to go home and earnestly
ask God's forgiveness; to hold the Bible in her
hand all night, and especially to beware of sleep-
ing with any string tied round her : then as soon
as the morning dawned she was to go "en
chemise" to the barn and tie up a bundle of
straw, and if the man appeared, to give him *that
knot.*

All this she did exactly, but could not sleep
for fear, and trembled like a leaf as the morning

dawned. Just as she had tied up the straw, the man appeared, and she threw it down saying it was the only knot she had tied that day. Then he suddenly grew large and terrible to look at, and his eyes were like fire; and he tried to fly at her and tear her to pieces; but as the Bible was in her bosom he could not hurt her, particularly as she fell on her knees and prayed. So he tore the bundle of straw in a thousand pieces and disappeared in fire and smoke.

She went back to her work and never asked for another holiday, except to see her mother and go to church; nor did she ever dance at the "son" again, you may be sure.

There are certain days in the year when these visitations of the evil one are most frequent. Le jour de St. Jean is one of them. But the Surveil de Noël, Christmas Eve, is the most dangerous night of all to be out in the dark, or any where except snug in bed or safe in church or chapel. Our churches, I am sorry to say, are not open on that eve, but the Wesleyans frequently remain in public prayer till midnight, or at least till past ten o'clock.

It is devoutly believed that at midnight all the cattle kneel down, whether in a stable or a field. And I have seen the dairy-maid put an extra "gerbe d'etrain" (bundle of straw) under the forefeet of the cows in anticipation of the genuflexion. It is not lawful to watch them. I was told that *once* a wicked man disbelieved the fact, and said that he would wait and see. He waited and he may have seen; but as he left the stable

K 3

the door slammed violently upon him and he fell dead on the threshold!

Also on this evening all water is turned into wine at the midnight hour, just as the clock strikes. No one likes to sit up so late in the country; but I remember one night having huge heaps of currants and raisins to stone for the Christmas pudding, and being unusually delayed, the clock struck. I immediately expressed a great desire to pump and see the wine, when I was forcibly prevented, and assured that a woman did so once, saying as she drank the water, "Tout eau est vin." "Oui mais tu es pres de ton fin," a voice answered, and she dropped down dead.

La Longue Veille.

The night before Christmas Eve is a very notable one in the country; it is called "La Longue Veille;" and poor indeed must be the cottage which has not a cup of vin brûlé, a piece of cheese, and a Guernsey galette for the Longue Veille. It is the merriest night of all the year, and gallons of wine are mulled by the bettermost farmers, which last them through the winter. As I never tasted any where such mulled wine as we make, I really think it will be kind to give the exact receipt, and recommend myself thus to your remembrance in every future Longue Veille; always under the stipulation that you abide by the good old Guernsey rule, which allows *one coffee cup* full of the vin brulè to every young person; two to married ladies, and three or at the utmost four to each gentleman. More than this is an unlawful excess and disgraces the offender.

Receipt for Guernsey Mulled Wine.

Some cloves and whole cinnamon ;
   An ounce of the last,
Of the first just one quarter;
   Boiled, but not boiled too fast,
In a quart of cold water
   To a dozen of wine ;
Take a pound of loaf sugar,
   Don't break it too fine ;
Let them stand both together
   While boiling the spice;
You can taste it to see
   That the sweetness is nice.
And the cloves and the cinnamon
   May simmer away,
If you're not in a hurry,
   One third of the day ;
It may then be poured into
   The wine, and is fit
To be warmed—but not boiled
   When you wish to drink it.

The last thing that I shall notice is the Guernsey Hallow'een, which is not on the 1st of November as it ought to be, but on the 21st of December, St. Thomas's Day. It is kept much after the Scotch fashion, and is a famous night for spells and visions, and unpleasant adventures with evil spirits. Men returning from their work in the evening have walked, and walked, and walked, always seeming to be near home, and never get-ting to their own door, till they have suddenly made a full stop, rubbed their eyes, and found themselves at Torteval or Rocquaine; or if it was a Torteval man, he has stumbled over the Roc de Guet at the Câtel.

Sometimes a great black dog will run rudely at a man and knock him down. Sometimes a white rabbit will go hopping before him till he is half crazed with fear. People do not like, on either the Surveil de Noêl or Le jour de St. Thomas, to wander about after dark. Nevertheless, the latter is a favourite day with young men and maidens; for then they perform all kinds of spells to find out who loves them, or "pour vè ki ki sera son homme," who is to be their husband.

St. Thomas has a spell of his own too; here it is:—Take a golden pippin, and eighteen new pins, which have never been used or stuck into paper; put nine in the eye, and nine in the stem, place it under your pillow, with the left garter round it, and get into bed backwards, saying,

> Le jour de St. Thomas
> Le plus court, le plus bas,
> Je prie Dieu journellement
> Qu'il me fasse voir, en dormant,
> Celui que sera mon amant,
> Et le pays et la contrèe
> Ou il fera sa demeurèe,
> Tel qu'il sera je l'aimerai.
> Ainsi soit il.

St. Thomas then bestows on the sleeper a dream of the future husband or wife.

There are many spells, and stories attached to

each, proving their efficacy; but I have recorded
enough of Guernsey superstitions for this little
book. Some are foolish enough, and I will not
defend them; neither do I hold them up to be
laughed at, for

" The sinner toyeth with witchcraft, thinking to delude
his fellow ;
But there be very spirits of evil, and what if they come
at his bidding ?" *Tupper's Proverbial Philosophy.*

Neither do I admire the spirit of this age of
reason, which turns so proudly away in its fancied
wisdom from all that is spiritual and supernatural.
The fairy lore and demonology of past times may
have concealed deep truth. Even Paganism was
an effort to realise the truth of a spiritual world
within this visible and earthly one. And in the
present day, some are found who fear not to ac-
knowledge a belief, and dwell upon it as a beautiful part of our Christian faith, " that the whole of
external nature may be regarded as a wonderful
assemblage of forms, or vases capable of a spiritual indwelling; by which means man, whose
daily life is conversant with these forms, is brought
into contact with the spiritual world."

Not only does a world of spirits exist close by
us, but our communication with it is, for the
most part, through the forms of external nature;
so that while we look round upon visible objects,
we are all the while hemmed in, and compassed
with invisible " powers, thrones, dominations,
principalities." (See " *Faber's Sights and Scenes
in Foreign Churches.*") We need not encourage

the popular superstitions; but we need not sweep
them all away as utterly absurd, and rush from the
weakness of credulity to the greater weakness
of scepticism,

CHAPTER VII.

CLIMATE.

WE are indebted to Dr. Hoskins for the following observations on the climate, &c. of Guernsey.

An account of the climate and diseases of this
island cannot be more appropriately prefaced than
by an extract from the highest authority on subjects of this kind. Sir James Clark, speaking of
the climate of the west and south-west of France,
states: "The islands of Guernsey and Jersey belong to this range of climate, and deserve some
notice, being occasionally resorted to as a winter
residence by invalids; and, when the cases are properly selected, often with advantage. In its physical qualities, the climate of these islands closely
resembles that which is common to the neighbouring coast of France."

With all deference to the above-quoted authority, it would perhaps be more correct to consider the climate of Guernsey as intermediate between that of the adjacent coast of France and
the south-western districts of England, than as
"closely resembling" either. It is, in fact, more
mild in winter than the former, and warmer at all
seasons than the latter: assimilating more closely

to Penzance, and possessing the same peculiarity
—warmth during the night. The island also possesses the singular advantage of affording luxuries
at a cheaper rate than the common necessaries of
life can be procured at most other places of vale-
tudinarian resort.

The temperature is subject to frequent, but not
extensive variations, seldom rising above 80° of
Fahrenheit, rarely falling below 38°; and never
remaining long stationary at or below freezing
point. The consequence is, that frost is not durable, and that snow never remains on the ground
many days, or rather hours. It was mentioned
erroneously, in a former publication, that the
temperature of Guernsey is three degrees inferior
to that of Jersey. The error arose from the want
of sufficient data for comparison: this want has
been since supplied by Dr. Hooper's valuable
work on the climate of Jersey. A more accurate
estimate thus formed between the two islands,
proves, that although Jersey is warmer in summer it is colder in winter. The mean annual
temperature of both appears to be as nearly as
possible equal, viz. rather above 53°. Dr. Hooper,
from careful observations made during five successive years, states, that the mean annual temperature of St. Helier's averaged 53°.06; that the
entire range of the thermometer was 62°; the two
extremes during the above-mentioned period being
88° and 26°.

The prevailing winds during the greater part of
the year are from the westward, as the shorn aspect of the trees in that direction of the coast in-

dicates. From the period of the vernal equinox
to the first week in May, keen easterly winds are
frequent; and when they occur, it behoves the
invalid to avoid incautious exposure; although
exercise in the open air, to which the inviting
aspect of the weather induces, may be indulged
in. The peculiar drying effect of this kind of atmosphere, imbibing every *halitus* that transudes
through the cutaneous pores, and a certain elec-
trical state inseparable from a long continuance
of easterly wind, combine to render this period of
the year insidious to those whose health is delicate, however delightful the clear sky and bracing
air may be to the robust.

To compensate, however, for these keen though
gentle breezes, the usual concomitants of a British spring, the Guernsey summer is delightfully
bland and temperate, and its delicious autumn
encroaches smilingly into the month of November. So fine is the weather generally for about
six weeks, at this season, that it has been pro-
verbially denominated, "Le petit été de Saint
Michel." From this period until January, the
weather is mild but variable, with high, though
not cold winds from the westward, accompanied
by rain; a combination called in the vernacular
"Temps de Guernesey." If there happens to be
any cold weather, brief intervals of it now occur
till late in February, when bland weather and
often warm sunshine prevail, until the middle of
March brings a return of the periodical gales.

An unfounded opinion is entertained of the
humidity and relaxing quality of the climate; but

the fact is, the annual number of days entirely wet are few, and we have authority for stating that, on the whole, less rain falls here than in the south-western parts of England. The rain which does fall is rather in the form of heavy showers succeeded by sunshine, than, as in some places, a continuation of wet for days together; these circumstances, and the absorbing nature of the soil, enable persons even in delicate health to take exercise throughout the winter.

Whether owing to the moderate range of temperature, or to whatever cause, Guernsey may be considered a decidedly healthy place, its only epidemics being those to which childhood chiefly is liable.

Intermittent fever as an endemic is now unknown, and all other diseases arising from malaria, including typhus, are of rare occurrence. It is a singular fact that immunity from ague is comparatively recent, coeval with the recovery of a considerable tract of land by the exclusion of an arm of the sea in the lower parishes. Here however, as in other low situations along the coast, bilious, or inflammatory remittent fever occasionally occurs in seasons when great heat has succeeded to much rain; owing to various circumstances, unnecessary to mention, these fevers occasionally assume a typhoid character. If the comparative freedom of this community from the visitation of malignant epidemics is to be ascribed to advantages of climate, the short duration and trifling ravages of infectious disorders, when they have appeared, may be attributed in a great mea-

L

sure, if not entirely, to the better order of dwellings, superior food, cleanliness, and clothing procured by the labouring classes; advantages which depend upon their careful, industrious, sober habits.

Scarlatina, measles, and other disorders incident to childhood are, in ordinary states of the atmosphere, mild and tractable: change however to severe weather, during their prevalence, imparts to them a congestive and more insidious character.

About twenty years ago, scarlet fever was very fatal, being accompanied by that peculiar ulceration of throat called by Bretonneau, *dipthérite;* and again, in the winter of 1838, it assumed a congestive form, complicated with inflammation of the lining membrane of the frontal and other sinuses. Defluxion of acrimonious fetid mucus took place from the nostrils, and almost all cases so affected terminated fatally by the supervention of cerebral symptoms.

Pleurisy, pneumonia, peritonitis, and indeed all acute diseases of the serous tissues and parenchymatous structures, are exceedingly rare in the town and its immediate vicinity. Sub-acute bronchitis, and other affections of the mucous membranes, are those which occur most frequently, as the active disorders requiring medical treatment. During the autumn, diarrhœa and muco-enteritis are common, owing partly to atmospheric influence, and partly to the quantity of fruit grown on the island, and imported from France.

The most predominant malady of all is that

proteiform disorder dyspepsia, popularly denominated "biliousness." It affects the peasantry
more commonly than the town residents, attribut-
able rather to the innutritious diet on which the
former subsist than to climate. Vesical calculus
is a rare phenomenon; and lithic acid deposits are
by no means so frequent as the prevalence of
dyspepsia would lead one to imagine. Disorders
accompanied by the phosphatic diathesis scarcely
ever fall under observation. Is it unfair to infer
from these facts, and from the absence of cal-
careous material in the geological formation, that
the place would not be unfavourable, nay, would
perhaps be positively beneficial, in cases of this
distressing description?

On the subject of pulmonary consumption, Dr.
Hooper's assertion as regards Jersey is equally
applicable to this island:—"The number of deaths
referable to this disease falls considerably below
the general average in other places." Of course
this remark applies to genuine tubercular phthisis
alone, and not to the host of diseases popularly
classed under the head "decline." Those who
may at first be startled by this assertion, will ac-
knowledge its truth when they reflect on the
denseness of the population in the principal towns
of the two islands, the intimate family connexions
which exist, and the constant intercourse taking
place between all classes, whereby each case that
occurs is matter of notoriety.

Having given a correct and as minute a sketch
as our limits permit, of the peculiarities of this
often misrepresented climate, we shall not seek to

extol its virtues as a universal panacea; but content ourselves with mentioning, from long personal experience, the modifications of disease in which it has proved beneficial.

The efficacy of our bland atmosphere in dry bronchial cough has long been acknowledged; it also proves serviceable in almost all cases of irritation in the air passages, whether accompanied by increased secretion or not. It is eminently beneficial in "dry asthma," not merely palliating the symptoms, but, in young persons especially, ultimately overcoming predisposition to the complaint. To discuss the merits of the climate in consumptive cases would be idle; change of atmosphere can only avail in the earliest dawn of the malady, and that change should be to a decidedly warm temperature. In the advanced stages of the complaint, advantages should indeed be great, which induced a patient to forego the comforts of home, increased as they are by present improved methods of regulating temperature, for the questionable benefits resulting from a change even to a more genial climate.

Persons from the northern and midland counties of England, without any specific disease, but enjoying (!), as it is called, delicate health, have latterly resorted to this island with manifest benefit; and after a sojourn of a year or two, without further medical interference than the regulation of habits, diet, &c., have been so much improved in health as to be enabled to return to their homes and resume their usual occupations. Perhaps this may have been caused by the mere

transition from a cold to a warmer atmosphere,—
from an inland to a maritime situation; and it
appears to be a good principle for adoption in re-
commending change of air, to send those who have
resided inland to the sea-coast, and *vice versâ.*

An eminent physician resident in one of the
above-named counties is so impressed with the
benefit that patients affected with strumous or
scrofulous affections of the joints, glands, &c.,
have derived from the change alluded to, that he has
expressed his intention of publishing observations
specifically on this subject. The intermediate
nature of the temperature likewise renders this
place an excellent transition-stage between England and the East or West Indies, for those whose
health has been impaired by long residence in
tropical climates.

If, as Sir James Clark says of Undercliff, more
conclusive evidence in favour of climate is furnished by the growth of exotic plants than by
thermometric results, we may appeal triumphantly
to our gardens and shrubberies, at all seasons, for
proofs of the superiority of a climate in which the
orange and the fig-tree mature their fruit in the
open air, the latter in exquisite perfection; where
trees of camellia japonica, of vast extent, are covered with blossoms from October to April; where
the myrtle, hydrangea, geranium, mimosa para-
doxa, " and other plants which grow with reluc-
tance, or not at all, in the mildest districts of
England, pass the winter without difficulty, and
emulate in summer the luxuriance they possess
in their native climates."

CHAPTER VIII.

LAWS AND GOVERNMENT, &c.

THIS island is governed by a singular mixture of Norman and English laws.

Soon after the establishment of the French monarchy, the Norman isles were placed under the direction of a Count. Count Loyescon was Governor in the reigns of Clotaire and Cherebent, about the year 560. At that time, and long afterwards, they were regulated by the feudal system.

King John, by a constitution which he gave them, appointed a Royal Court, which was empowered to judge all causes arising in the island. Appeals were to be made from the feudal Courts to this new institution; which, by its encroachments, soon deprived the former of most of their powers.

Since that time the Sovereign of England has been acknowledged in these islands as the supreme authority, in the same degree that they once owned allegiance to the Dukes of Normandy; but the power exercised is neither unlimited or despotic, for the island preserves its privileges of judging by its own laws—of a free trade with all countries—and of total exemption from *taxes*. The sovereign of England cannot make a new law, or abolish any of the established customs; though he reserves to himself the final decision in all civil cases where appeal is made from the judgment of the court.

The Legislative Power

Is vested in the hands of the States, which consist of the Administrative States, and the Elective States.

The Administrative States are composed of

The Bailiff and twelve Jurats . .	13
The Rectors of Parishes, or beneficed Clergy	8
The King's Procureur . . .	1
One Constable from each parish . .	10
	32

This body is properly a general council of the island, wherein every inhabitant is supposed to be represented, and which is or ought to be the sole legislative authority.

The Administrative States are convened by a written notice of convocation, issued by the Bailiff, and communicated to every member of the body, with a notice of the subjects to be discussed.

The Elective States are composed of

The Bailiff and twelve Jurats . .	13
Rectors of Parishes	8
The King's Procureur . . .	1
Two Constables from each Parish .	20
Twenty Douzeniers from St. Peter's Port	20
Sixteen ditto from the Vale Parish	16
Twelve from each of the other eight Parishes	96
	174

This body is assembled only to elect Jurats and the King's Sheriff.

The Bailiff is elected by the Sovereign, and a

salary of £300 per ann., payable out of the local
Crown revenue, is attached to the office.   The
Jurats are, as we have seen, elected by the States,
and receive no salary ; it is understood that they
serve for life, the consent of the States, and the
sanction of an order in council, being requisite to
their discharge.   They are chosen from amongst
the most distinguished, discreet, wise, loyal, and
rich of the inhabitants, no matter what may have
been their previous pursuits.

The Officers attached to the Court are an
Attorney General, a Solicitor or Advocate General,
a Greffier or Clerk, a Prevost, a Serjeant; and
there are also Six Advocates, who are appointed
by the Bailiff and Jurats.

These officers administer justice three times a
week in Term time, and once a week out of Term,
or oftener if required.   There are three Terms in
the year.

The first or Christmas Term begins on the first
Monday after the 15th of January.

The second or Easter Term, on the first Monday
after the 15th of May.

The third or Michaelmas Term, on the first
Monday after the 29th of September; and each of
them continues six weeks.   This Court has power
of life and death, except in cases of treason, coin-
ing, or actual assault upon the Bailiff, when a
direct application must be made to Her Majesty's
Government.

On the first day or opening of each Term, called
the Chief Pleas, bye-laws and ordinances are
made, which have the immediate effect of law.

The Mobiliare Courts, in which pleas are determined for moveables and chattels, common debts sued for, and executions obtained by creditors, are held on Mondays; the lower parishes, viz. St. Peter's Port, St. Sampson's, and the Vale, being attended to one week, and the upper and remaining parishes on the following Monday, and so on alternately.

The Plaids d'Heritage, or Court of Heritage, is of great antiquity. It must be held by the Bailiff and three of the Jurats at least, and takes place on every other Tuesday in the Term, beginning with the second Tuesday. In this court are determined all suits relative to personal property.

The Criminal Court is held on Saturday or Thursday, when police cases are disposed of; and the Admiralty Court, which takes into consideration the decision of maritime contracts, freights, insurance, and all cases of great urgency, particularly arrests, whether of person or effects, is also held on Saturday.

The Tenure of Property.

Farms are sold not for a certain sum of money, as in England, but for so many quarters of wheat to be paid annually; the relations of the proprietor may, within a year after the first agreement, claim the property, and may have it on paying the amount for which it has been parted with. The following are some of the local customs referring to this point.

Renunciation and Cession.—A person who, from losses in trade or other unavoidable calamity, finds himself insolvent, may avail himself of the privilege of *Cession;* which is done by appearing in open court, declaring his renunciation of all his property, and swearing that he will deliver all his moveables (his clothes, bed, and arms excepted) to and for the benefit of his creditors, and that if Providence should enable him hereafter to pay his just debts, he will do so.   In ancient times a person thus renouncing wore a green cap and divested himself of his girdle; but this humiliating act has been discontinued for some years.

Saisie.—This is a remedy granted to a creditor when his debtor becomes insolvent.   There are three kinds of *Saisie:* the *Saisie Mobilière,* when, before the renunciation, the creditor has obtained an act of the court, and takes possession of the debtor's estate, the revenue of which he applies towards the liquidating of his own claim, the debtor still retaining the property of the estate: the *Saisie Hérédital,* when the debtor has renounced, or by process of law has been forced to give up his estate in favour of his creditors, of which the said *Saisie* becomes administrator without prejudice to his own personal claims.   The *Saisie* becomes *Propriétaire,* when he who held the *Saisie Mobilière,* or *Hérédital,* has by some act which has been deemed binding, made it his own; or when, in the regular process, one of the creditors has accepted the *Saisie.*   In either case the *Saisie Propriétaire* is in the place of the original debtor, and answerable for all the debts which can be proved.

Retraites.—The origin of this custom seems to

have been the Mosaic law. When any person alienates his inheritance by sale or rent, if any part of the consideration for such assignment is paid, or agreed to be paid in money, the next of kindred, and if he or she refuses, or neglects to claim his or her right, the next in rotation, in like manner, to the seventh degree of consanguinity, may at any time do so, until the purchaser is appointed by the court, at one of the fixed days regularly held for such purposes, or within one year, if no such appropriation has taken place, upon payment of the sum *bonâ fide* paid upon the purchase.

Land may not, when the owner leaves descendants, be disposed of by will, but must descend to the heirs-at-law; or in default of these to the King or Lord of the Manor. A father cannot by will give any advantage to one child over another, even in reference to his personal property. A husband acquires no permanent right over his wife's estate; if she leaved issue, he enjoys the property for life; but should she die without having had a child born alive, the estate, immediately on her death, reverts to the heirs-at-law, in the same manner as if she had never been married.

With regard to the division of property amongst brothers and sisters, a new code of laws has been lately established, drawn up by the States, and confirmed by her Majesty in Council, which, in most cases, is decidedly preferable to the old one; only that the power of Willing should be much extended.

ARTICLE 1.—The right of the sons to the *vingtième*, or twentieth part of the estate, is abolished. The eldest son's right to the *préciput** shall be continued, subject, however, to the modifications stated in the Articles that follow.

ART. 2.—In successions to real property in a direct line, when sons and daughters succeed together, they shall share, after the *préciput* of the eldest son has been taken, the sons two-thirds, the daughters one-third; excepting in cases where, by this method, the portion of a son would exceed double that of a daughter, in which case the portion of the sons shall be reduced to double the portion of each of the daughters; excepting also in cases where, by this method, the portion of a daughter would exceed that of a son, in which latter cases the sons and daughters shall share in equal portions.

ART. 3.—In successions to personal property, the eldership shall be one-seventh of the household furniture, after the third of the widow has been taken; and also all family portraits, and pieces of plate, or other objects given to the father, or other ancestors, by public bodies.

ART. 4.—In direct or lineal successions, when there shall be only daughters to share, the youngest one will make the lots, after which they shall choose according to seniority.

ART. 5.—The *préciput* of the eldest son shall not extend beyond a single enclosure, notwithstanding such enclosure may not contain the quantity of land usually given as *préciput*, which is from fourteen to twenty-two perches.

---

* *Préciput* means eldership.

ART. 6.—When an enclosure on which the eldest son has taken his *préciput* shall not contain one-third of the land to be divided, the said *préciput* included, the Douzeniers of the parish shall assign him, should he require it, besides the said enclosure, land to the extent of the said third, in such part of the estate as they shall think proper. And the said eldest son shall remunerate his co-heirs for the value of the said third, (the *préciput* excepted), according to an estimate that shall be made by the said Douzeniers.

ART. 7.—The eldest son shall take no *préciput* on the estate of the survivor of his father or mother, unless he have caused a valuation to be made, by the Douzeniers of the parish, of the *préciput* already taken by him on the estate of his first deceased parent, at the period when he took it; and he shall bring back the said value, that it may be divided, if he intends taking the second *préciput*. The valuation shall be made by the said Douzeniers, both in rents and in money, so that the said eldest son may have the choice to bring back the value in either way. If the value be brought back in rents, those rents shall be assignable during forty years, in the same manner as all other rents created to equalize lots among co-heirs. A grandson who shall already have taken a *préciput* on the estate of his father and mother, may always take, in the succession of a grandfather or grandmother, the *préciput* to which his father (if he was the eldest son) would have had a right, in the same manner, and on the same conditions, with respect to the co-heirs of his said father. And it shall be optional with him to divide it with his consanguine brothers or sisters, or to keep it himself, on bringing back the value of that which he already possesses.

M

ART. 8.—The houses, buildings, and lands, situated within the barriers of the town, shall be divided between co-heirs in a direct line, in the manner indicated in Article 2, without a *préciput* being allowed to the eldest son. The limits of the barriers shall be traced as follows:—All properties found to the left of the line, traced as far as the sea, will be included in the barriers, viz. the line to commence on the sea shore at the Long-store, passing in front of the said building, taking the road leading to St. John's Church,—through the Amballes, as far as the road leading to the Cotils,—through the Cotils-road to the east of Mr. Tupper's estate, and to the south of Castle Carey,—then descending by Vauxlorens pump as far as the south-west wall of the Town Hospital,—following the line of the said wall as far as Hospital-street, ascending that street,—passing in front of the principal entrance of St. James's Church, —up Grange-road as far as Vauvert-road,—by the top of Vauvert to the west of the house belonging to the heirs of the late Wm. Le Cocq, Esq.,—descending the lane leading to the Petites Fontaines to the east of the land belonging to Mr. J. Crick. From this point the line will cross the lands in a straight direction as far as Mount-Durant pump,—and from thence, also in a straight direction, to the east angle of the Charoterie pond,—then ascend Park-lane steps, descend Vardes-road, and through Havelet-road as far as the sea.

ART. 9.—Properties situated within the barriers of the town, becoming divisible in direct successions, shall previously be valued by the Douzeniers of the town, and each of them forming a lot with its dependencies, shall be successively offered, at the price of the valuation, first to the sons, and afterwards to the daughters, according to seniority. If the eldest son chooses the first lot, the second shall be first offered to the second son, and so on in this manner. If the eldest son refuses the first lot, he shall have the choice of the second, and so on in this manner. Such of the lots as are refused by all the co-heirs at this price, shall be sold by public auction for account of the co-heirs.

ART. 10.—Married daughters shall have a right to share in the successions of their father and mother, provided they bring back to the division the capital they may have received from the parent whose succession is about to be shared. But it shall always be optional with them to retain their capital, and refuse to share in the succession.

ART. 11.—In collateral successions to *propres*, neither males nor their descendants shall exclude females or their descendants; but the relatives of both sexes belonging to the line whence the property descends, shall divide the estate by branches, in the same proportion as in successions in the direct line.

ART. 12.—In collateral successions to personal property, and purchased real property, neither males nor their descendants shall exclude females nor their descendants in parity of degree; but the nearest of kin to the deceased, in parity of degree, both males and females, shall share the property in the same proportions as property of this nature, whether personal or real, would be shared in successions in the direct line; and representation of degree shall be allowed when nephews and nieces shall come to the succession of an uncle or aunt with the brothers and sisters of the deceased, and not otherwise, in which case the said nephews and nieces shall subdivide among themselves, in the same manner, that portion of the succession which would have fallen to their father or mother, had he or she been alive.

ART. 13.—Ascendants, having no descendants living, shall inherit the personal property and purchased real property of the last of their descendants. In ascending successions, the father shall be preferred to the mother, and the paternal to the maternal line in parity of degree. In the same cases as above, the ascendants shall also inherit respectively the inherited real property of their line only. The father shall, in all cases, have the right to take from the estate of his child, deceased without descendants, such advances in anticipation of his own death as he may have made him, and for which he has obtained an acknowledgment in writing, or an act of court stating the advance so made.

ART. 14.—Every person leaving no descendants shall be at liberty to dispose by will, or by gift, to take effect at his death, of the whole of his purchased real property; and also in the same manner of his inherited real property, provided he have no relatives in the second degree, inclusively belonging to the line whence that inherited real property has been derived.

ART. 15.—The will of the real property shall be made distinct from that of the personal property.

ART. 16.—Every instrument giving real property to be enjoyed at the donor's death, and every legacy of real property, shall be signed by the donor or testator, in the presence of two jurats of the Royal Court,—or before the bailiff and two jurats in the case of a wife under coverture, whose oath shall be required. The instrument thus authenticated may nevertheless be changed or modified at any time by another similar instrument; it may even be destroyed, without any formality, by the donor or testator.

ART. 17.—Every will of real property may be deposited by the testator himself at the Greffe of the Royal Court, on paying two shillings and sixpence to the greffier. The testator may require the will to be put under a sealed envelope; in which case this envelope shall be put in presence of the greffier, who shall assure himself that the instrument thus secured is really the will of the party depositing it. This will shall at any time be delivered up, without payment, on the demand of the testator.

ART. 18.—Any person shall be at liberty to obtain permission from the Royal Court, on furnishing proof of the decease of an individual, to examine at the Greffe whether the deceased has deposited there a will. For the reading of the will, should any be found, the greffier shall charge two shillings; after which any person may have the will read on paying one shilling to the greffier.

ART. 19.—After the decease of a testator, the legatees, or one of them, shall obtain permission from the Royal Court to cause the will to be registered on the book of contracts, which permission shall be granted after proof of the said decease, without prejudice to the rights of others.

ART. 20.—After the registration of a will, the greffier may give copy thereof to any one, as of a contract, and at the same cost; but the original shall always remain deposited at the Greffe.

ART. 21.—In the event of a universal legacy, that is to say, when the testator shall have given to one or several persons the whole of his real property disposable by will, or the residue thereof, if there are other legacies, the universal or residuary legatees shall be entitled to take possession of the entire real property disposable by will, without being obliged to ask delivery thereof from the heirs.

ART. 22.—Legatees, to whom the testator shall have bequeathed a given share of the real property which the law allowed him to dispose of by will, shall be bound to ask the division thereof from the heirs or residuary legatees, as the case may be, which latter shall be entitled to seize or possess themselves of the property.

ART. 23.—The special legatee, that is to say, one to whom a definite object shall have been bequeathed, shall be bound to ask the delivery thereof from the heirs, or residuary legatees, as the case may be.

ART. 24.—The special legatee shall not be liable to anything beyond the real charges to which the property bequeathed to him was specially held, unless the other properties of the estate should be insufficient to pay the testator's debts.

ART. 25.—Universal legatees shall be liable, in connection with the heirs of the residuary legatees, for their proportion of such real charges as are due on the whole estate generally, and to which no separate part thereof is specifically liable. They shall, in the same manner, be liable for their proportion of the excess of personal debts, after all the personal property of the estate has been applied to the discharge of the same.

ART. 26.—Within six months from his being put in possession, the legatee shall deliver to each of the rent-holders to which the property bequeathed to him is indebted, a copy, under the seal of the bailiwick, of the will, or of the part thereof that concerns him. If he is not the sole universal or residuary legatee, he must deliver a copy, thus authenticated, of the "*Bille de Partage*," or other document, correctly defining the part of the estate bequeathed to him, and the debts due upon it. In default of his doing so within the said period, the heirs, in order to discharge themselves of their responsibility towards the rent-holders, may make the delivery of the said instruments, and, in that case, shall recover all the expenses they may be at, and half the amount thereof besides, from the legatee. The rent-holders themselves may also, after the same period, procure the said instruments, and exercise the same right of recovery against the legatee.

ART. 27.—The right of redemption is abolished, with regard to all real property disposed of by judicial public auctions.

ART. 28.—A married woman shall have no hypothecation for her dower, on any part of the estate of her husband's ancestor, (notwithstanding he may have consented to the marriage), unless the said ancestor have expressly granted her the said hypothecation by a special judicial contract.

ART. 29.—A mother, in the same manner as a father, shall not be at liberty to give, by will, to one child more than to another. Fathers and mothers may order the proportion of their married daughters to be placed in trust, and the dividend to be paid to such daughters during their coverture,—well understood that, if they survive their said husbands, the capital shall be transferred to the said daughters, and that if they die before their husbands, the capital shall be transferred to their heirs, unless the said daughters should, in cases where this is allowed, have willed away the said capital.

Art. 30.—Articles 1, 2, and 8 shall not apply to families in which the eldest of the sons, living at the opening of the succession, shall have attained the age of fourteen years when the present law is promulgated. Article 7 shall not apply to eldest sons having attained the age of fourteen years at the said period.

MILITARY AUTHORITY.

In ancient times the government of this island was committed to persons of the highest rank and trust in the realm, sometimes to princes of the blood royal; at which period both civil and military power were vested in the hands of the same individual, who, however, employed a deputy, and usually left the administration of justice in his hands, with the title of Bailiff or Guardian. The Governorship was then a grant of the islands, with all their revenues, for a certain number of years, or a lifetime. They were granted thus by Richard I. to his brother John; by Henry V. to his brother the Duke of Bedford; by Henry VI. to his uncle the Duke of Gloucester; and the title of Governor was also borne by the Earl of Salisbury, Lord de Grey, Otho de Grandison, and other nobles, until 1672; when those who received it ceased to reside in the island, and governed by Lieutenant-Governors.

In later years this high office became merely nominal, and entirely separate from the judicial authority; the governors received the crown revenues, and did not interfere with the local powers at all. Sir William Keppel was the last governor; and since his death, in 1834, the governorship has been abolished, and the revenues placed at the disposal of the Lords of the Treasury.

The present Lieutenant-Governor, General Napier, the distinguished author of the *"History of the Peninsular War,"* is appointed by the Crown as Commander-in-Chief of the forces in Guernsey, Alderney, and Sark; he grants commissions to officers in the militia, has the patronage of all the parochial livings, and a deliberative voice, but no vote, in the meetings of the States, and also of the Chief Pleas of the Court.

Table-money is allowed to the Lieutenant-Governor, and four militia officers as aides-de-camp. General Napier does not reside at Government House, but at Havilland Hall, on St. Andrew's Road, the seat of Colonel de Havilland.

CHAPTER IX.

AGRICULTURE AND FLORICULTURE.

THE arable, pasture, orchard and garden land, are estimated at about 10,000 English acres, divided into very small farms, containing from about thirty to a hundred vergées. The Guernsey vergée is forty perches; and two vergées and a half are rather more than one English acre. The extreme neatness and economy of the land will be remarked by the stranger: not a foot of ground is lost, even in the hedges, which supply fuel in the beautiful flowering furze, and which are frequently planted with shrubs, or kept as a flower bank, when no other ground can be spared. The usual rotation of crops is as follows: wheat, barley, clover, and parsneps, which order has been preserved for centuries; the latter crop is preceded by a great feast, called *La grande Kerrue*, or *Charrue*, which takes place in February and March, when the farmers plough for parsneps; and, as they would not upon any consideration give up or *improve* the heavy plough which requires so many horses to draw it, it is customary to invite the neighbouring farmers, each of whom brings either bullocks or horses to assist in the arduous task; the occasion is quite a festival, and the day one of rare gossiping and merriment. It is not at all unusual to see two yoke of oxen and twelve horses to the great plough; whilst a smaller one, with a less number, follows in another track; and the sight is a strange one to the English farmer.

The land is generally manured with sea-weed and weed-ashes; sea-sand and salt are also sometimes employed. The soil is, in most parts, a fine gravelly or sandy loam, abundantly fertile, and well watered with remarkably pure streams and springs; and the average crops are more abundant than in most countries.

Wheat.

In England the average produce of wheat, according to Young, Cobbett, and various agricultural societies, is from twenty-one to twenty-three or four bushels per acre. In Guernsey it is *thirty-three;* and it has been ascertained upon the highest authority, (that of our late bailiff), that fifty-four and *fifty-five* bushels have been the produce of an acre of ground at St. Martin's.

Hay-crops average three tons and a half, English weight, per acre.

Parsneps, which are very successful here, yield about twenty-two tons per English acre.

Of potatoes, the average crop is fourteen tons to the English acre, but many fields are known to have yielded the astonishing quantity of twenty tons per acre.

Orchards.

The orchards are very productive; but little cider is now made in the island; it is the principal beverage of the peasantry and farmers.

Many varieties of the melon ripen here ; the superiority of the Chaumontel pears is well known, and they are sent to England in great quantities. Fig-trees and vines bear even the wintry winds without shelter, and produce abundantly; but the latter only come to perfection in a greenhouse. The grapes which have been exported, particularly some grown by Savary Brock, Esq., and presented by him to Her Majesty, were certainly never surpassed in size and flavour in any climate.

Frederick Mansell, Esq., of the Vauxbellets, in St. Andrew's parish, has grapes which vie with any yet produced, whether in the size of the berry or the flavour of the fruit. (This estate is noted for its beautiful horned cattle).

The stranger has only to visit our fruit-market, in any of the summer months, to see how abundantly we are supplied with the best kinds of small fruit; the finest flavoured strawberries being often sold at a penny per pound, and currants at twopence per pound.

Floriculture.

In Guernsey, every cottager is a gardener, every village almost is a shrubbery, where the most delicate and tender shrubs grow luxuriantly; geraniums run up the cottage walls, supporting their bright scarlet clusters on myrtle boughs; the beautiful "fuchsia coccinea" lives hardily side by side with the "verbena tryphilla," which in England is a greenhouse plant, and *here* becomes a tree of twelve or even eighteen feet in height, with its fragrant branches spreading out on all sides, reaching to the ground.

The "magnolia grandiflora" blossoms freely in many parts of the island; but no where so luxuriantly as at Woodlands, in the Câtel parish, where it is a noble tree, twenty feet in height, and eight feet in girth, covered in the month of September with magnificent flowers. Hydrangeas are common all over the country; myrtles and roses cover every cottage wall; and the "amaryllis sarniensis," or Guernsey lily, is too well known to be described. Every garden has a bed of these lovely flowers, and in many places they increase so rapidly as to overrun the garden ground.

The florist will be highly gratified by attending our horticultural shows, which take place several times during the summer, and are held in the fish-market, where fruits, flowers, and vegetables are displayed to great advantage.

Amongst the latter, it may surprise the stranger to observe the luxuriance of our cabbage-plants; one species of which attains to the height of six or eight feet, and, as it most commonly grows in orchards, may be seen resting its round, heavy head on the topmost branches of a dwarf apple-tree; the stalks of these cabbages are rarely straight, unless thus supported. They are finest in St. Andrew's parish and in Sark.

CHAPTER X.

TAXATION—QUEEN'S REVENUES—HARBOUR DUES—CURRENCY, ETC.

TAXATION.

THERE is one regular tax upon the natives of the island, in which every one is laid under contribution according to his means, and is assessed not only for the value of whatever he may possess in the island, but also for the amount of what he may hold in the British or Foreign funds; the only exception allowed being that of real property in England, upon which it is presumed

N

that a tax is already paid. It is essentially a tax on realized property, and not upon industry,—unproductive capital being assessed, whilst pensions, salaries, professional incomes, and half-pay are exempted.

The standard by which it is measured is termed a " quarter," from wheat having been the original standard of value. A "quarter" is now valued at 20*l.*, and, taking one year with another, the annual tax for parochial purposes may be computed at sixpence per quarter. This covers *every* demand; and no one is annoyed for poor-rate, lighting, watching, window or house tax.

All monies required for general purposes are raised by an impost on spirituous liquors.

THE QUEEN'S REVENUE.

This consists of the great tithes of all corn, grain, and flax, the growth of the island, and in some parts the champart is also levied; first, the tenth sheaf for tithe, and the eleventh for champart when the fief belongs to the crown. *Champart* implies that part reserved by the lords of the manors and fiefs, by way of chief rent, which is generally let out or farmed at certain rates by private individuals.

The chief rents, and rents paid in corn and money, with the customs, anchorage, tonnage on vessels, wrecks at sea, amercements of court, forfeitures in estates, goods, chattels, &c., constitute the chief revenues of the crown in Guernsey.

Queen's Receiver—Daniel Tupper, Esq.

CHURCH REVENUES.

The church revenues consist of the small tithes and champart, together with norvals or tithe on lands, brought under cultivation since the Roman Catholic exactions, and they are different in almost every parish.

St. Peter's Port.—A seventh of tithe and champart.
St. Martin's.— Do. do. do.
The Catel.—Ninth of tithe, or full tithes of a certain portion of the parish.
The Forest.—A ninth of tithes and champart.
Torteval.—A third of tithe.
St. Saviour's.—The norvals and tenths; about 600 sheaves.
St. Andrew's.—A fourth of tithe and champart.
St. Peter's-in-the-Wood.—A third of tithe.
The Vale.—Five of the King's tithe only.
St. Sampson's.—Five of both.

The rectors have also a full disme or tithe of all the apples, pears, cider, honey, calves, colts, pigs, lambs, geese, and fish; but no tithe whatever is due, either to the crown or rector, for hay, clover, lucerne, potatoes, parsneps, cabbage, or other vegetables.

HARBOUR DUES.

Vessels registered in this island, and belonging to natives or to persons naturalized by ordinances of the Royal Court, *pay nothing;* all others pay as follows:—

					Anchorage.		Chainage.	
					s.	*d.*	*s.*	*d.*
All	vessels	under	10 tons	··	0	6	0	6
„	from 10 to	20 do.	.....		1	0	1	0
„	„	20 to	30 do.	.....	1	6	1	6
„	„	30 to	40 do.	.....	2	0	2	0
„	„	40 to	50 do.	.....	3	0	3	0
„	„	50 to	60 do.	.....	4	0	4	0
„	„	60 to	80 do.	.....	5	0	5	0
„	„	80 to	100 do.	.....	6	0	6	0
„	„	100 to	150 do.	.....	7	0	7	0
„	„	150 to	200 do.	.....	7	6	7	6
„	„	250 to	300 & above		9	0	9	0

The anchorage and chainage are paid by every vessel coming into harbour; the chainage is not paid by those who do not come into it.

St. Peter's Port.—All wines landed here, whether for inhabitants or for strangers' account, pay a duty of fifteen *sous* per ton to the States.

St. Sampson's Harbour.—In virtue of her Majesty's Order in Council, July 31, 1839,

1. Twopence per ton on all stones, or other goods, loaded on board of all vessels belonging to the island or otherwise, in the parishes of St. Sampson and the Vale; the said twopence per ton to be payable by the owners or masters of the said vessels.

2. One penny per ton on all stones loaded for exportation, within the said parishes, in any boat or vessel, to be payable by the merchant or other person loading the said stones.

All vessels clearing out, *whether registered or not,* pay two shillings for the pass; which dues belong to the lieutenant-governor.

TONNAGE DUES.

British vessels *not registered here* pay 6*d.* per ton for all goods landed and loaded.

Foreign vessels, having treaties of reciprocity, pay 6*d.* per ton on the tonnage of vessels measured as British tonnage. All other foreign vessels pay 2*s.* per ton, on the goods loaded and unloaded.

British vessels coming here from any French port pay 6*d.* per ton on the tonnage of the vessel.

Fishing vessels and yachts pay no dues of any kind, excepting the pass.

Three doubles (three-eighths of a penny) are paid per quarter on all coals landed here.

Vessels exporting coals pay no tonnage dues.

CURRENCY.

The legal currency of the island, or that in which sales of real property, and fines attached to the infraction of local laws, are stated in title-deeds and in ordinances, is the old currency of towns in Normandy, now called Tournois currency, and having but a nominal existence.

Of this money 14*l.* are equal to 1*l.* sterling; but

The Guernsey Circulating Medium

is the modern French coin : five-franc pieces, two-franc pieces, francs and half-francs, with a local-specie called *doubles,* of which eight go to a penny English.

N 3

Twenty-four francs are made to represent one pound sterling.

The real exchange at par between the French coin and British sterling, being, however, 25 francs 22 centimes to the pound, of $1\frac{1}{2}$ franc more than is required to constitute a pound sterling, Guernsey currency, it follows that there is a difference of 12*d.* in the pound, or 5 per cent., between a Guernsey pound sterling, and a British pound sterling. Hence there is in Guernsey a constant premium in favour of British sterling, varying according to the scarcity of bills on London, from 5, $5\frac{1}{2}$, or 6 per cent.

Banking Companies.

Guernsey Banking Company, 29, High Street.

Guernsey Commercial Banking Company, 22, High Street.

The chief business of these companies is to draw and cash bills on London and Paris, &c.; to discount promissory notes, and advance money.

The banks are open every day (Sundays and holidays excepted) from ten o'clock in the morning until three in the afternoon.

Money Table.

The following Table for converting Francs into Sterling will be found very useful to strangers.

Fr.	£	s.	d.	Fr.	£	s.	d.	Fr.	£	s.	d.	Fr.	£	s.	d.
1 .	0	0	10	37 .	1	10	10	73 .	3	0	10	109 .	4	10	10
2 .	0	1	8	38 .	1	11	8	74 .	3	1	8	110 .	4	11	8
3 .	0	2	6	39 .	1	12	6	75 .	3	2	6	111 .	4	12	6
4 .	0	3	4	40 .	1	13	4	76 .	3	3	4	112 .	4	13	4
5 .	0	4	2	41 .	1	14	2	77 .	3	4	2	113 .	4	14	2
6 .	0	5	0	42 .	1	15	0	78 .	3	5	0	114 .	4	15	0
7 .	0	5	10	43 .	1	15	10	79 .	3	5	10	115 .	4	15	10
8 .	0	6	8	44 .	1	16	8	80 .	3	6	8	116 .	4	16	8
9 .	0	7	6	45 .	1	17	6	81 .	3	7	6	117 .	4	17	6
10 .	0	8	4	46 .	1	18	4	82 .	3	8	4	118 .	4	18	4
11 .	0	9	2	47 .	1	19	2	83 .	3	9	2	119 .	4	19	2
12 .	0	10	0	48 .	2	0	0	84 .	3	10	0	120 .	5	0	0
13 .	0	10	10	49 .	2	0	10	85 .	3	10	10	125 .	5	4	2
14 .	0	11	8	50 .	2	1	8	86 .	3	11	8	130 .	5	8	4
15 .	0	12	6	51 .	2	2	6	87 .	3	12	6	135 .	5	12	6
16 .	0	13	4	52 .	2	3	4	88 .	3	13	4	140 .	5	16	8
17 .	0	14	2	53 .	2	4	2	89 .	3	14	2	145 .	6	0	10
18 .	0	15	0	54 .	2	5	0	90 .	3	15	0	150 .	6	5	0
19 .	0	15	10	55 .	2	5	10	91 .	3	15	10	155 .	6	9	2
20 .	0	16	8	56 .	2	6	8	92 .	3	16	8	160 .	6	13	4
21 .	0	17	6	57 .	2	7	6	93 .	3	17	6	165 .	6	17	6
22 .	0	18	4	58 .	2	8	4	94 .	3	18	4	170 .	7	1	8
23 .	0	19	2	59 .	2	9	2	95 .	3	19	2	175 .	7	5	10
24 .	1	0	0	60 .	2	10	0	96 .	4	0	0	180 .	7	10	0
25 .	1	0	10	61 .	2	10	10	97 .	4	0	10	185 .	7	14	2
26 .	1	1	8	62 .	2	11	8	98 .	4	1	8	190 .	7	18	4
27 .	1	2	6	63 .	2	12	6	99 .	4	2	6	195 .	8	2	6
28 .	1	3	4	64 .	2	13	4	100 .	4	3	4	200 .	8	6	8
29 .	1	4	2	65 .	2	14	2	101 .	4	4	2	300 .	12	10	0
30 .	1	5	0	66 .	2	15	0	102 .	4	5	0	400 .	16	13	4
31 .	1	5	10	67 .	2	15	10	103 .	4	5	10	500 .	20	16	8
32 .	1	6	8	68 .	2	16	8	104 .	4	6	8	600 .	25	0	0
33 .	1	7	6	69 .	2	17	6	105 .	4	7	6	700 .	29	3	4
34 .	1	8	4	70 .	2	18	4	106 .	4	8	4	800 .	33	6	8
35 .	1	9	2	71 .		19	2	107 .	4	9	2	900 .	37	10	0
36 .	1	10	0	72 .	3	0	0	108 .	4	10	0	1000 .	41	13	4

PRICES CURRENT IN GUERNSEY.

The great influx of strangers during late years has certainly rendered Guernsey a more expensive place than it was formerly, and some things will be seen in the following scale nominally to average about the London prices; such as meat, which varies from 5d. to 8d. per lb.; though, in reality, it is cheaper, from the difference of weight; the Guernsey lb. being one-eighth more than the English lb.; and this should be remembered in making household calculations.

Groceries, wines, spirits, &c., are very considerably cheaper; so are oats, beans, and other food for horses, hay excepted; which, besides the absence of all duty on horses, carriages, or groom— and no toll-gates, the roads being kept in excellent repair by the States—render the island still a more economical place of residence than could be found in any part of England with the same advantages of situation and good society.

House rent varies from 25l. to 50l. per annum, unfurnished, with garden and greenhouse; or, from 50l. to 100l. furnished,—of course, tax free.

PRICES OF WINES PER DOZEN (BOTTLES NOT INCLUDED).

French Red Wines.

Claret, Château Margaux .... } 50s.
  ,,   La Fitte, La Tour ....
  ,,   La Rose, Leoville .... 42s.
  ,,   La Tour de Carnet.................. } 36s.
  ,,   Lafou Rochet, Liversan ....
  ,,   St. Julien, St. Estephe.. .... 24s. 30
  ,,   S. Emilion 15s. 20
  ,,   Bas Medoc 8s. 12

Hermitage....... 48
Côte Rôtie................. 44
Burgundy, Chambertin 48
,, Baume 36
,, Moulin à Vent. 54
Cornas 30
Château Neuf du Pape 12s. 14
Tavel...... ....12s. 15
Roussillon, doux 10s. 12
,, sec ... .10s. 12
,, Masdeu 10s. 12
St. George.... ....8s. 10
Montagne 7s. 8

French White Wines.

Champaign, White and Pink.. ....36s. 50s.
,, Pints 26
Hermitage.... 48
Château Grillé.... 36
Haut Sauterne.. ....30s. 36
Haut Barsac.... ....30s. 36
Sauterne 24
Barsac 24
Chablis.... 30
Grave 12s. 20
Muscat de Rivesaltes 26
,, Frontignan.................... 12s. 18
,, Beziers 10
Roussillon, doux 8s. 10s. 12
,, sec 8s. 10

Portugal and other Wines.

Madeira, Lond. Part. E. I. ....32s.
,, ,, old 28
,, ,, 2nd 20

Madeira, Fine Malmsey 36
Port, 1st 24*s.* 26
  ,,   2nd 16*s.* 20
Ampurdam 8*s.* 10
Benicarlo 8*s.* 10
Hock 44
Sherry, 1st 26*s.* 35
  ,,   2nd 20
  ,,   Malaga....................8*s.* 10*s.* 12
Mountain..........................10*s.*_12
Teneriffe 12*s.* 16
Marsala..........................10*s.* 12*s.* 16
Lisbon 18

Liqueurs.

Crême de Noyau .... ⎫
  ,,   Noyau rouge .... ⎪
  ,,   Fine Orange............... ⎪
  ,,   Citron .... ⎪
  ,,   Mocha.................... ⎬ 3*s.* per bottle.
  ,,   Cinnamome .... ⎪
  ,,   Framboise .... ⎪
  ,,   des Barbadoes............. ⎪
Parfait Amour...................... ⎪
Ratafia de Cinq Fruits .... ⎪
Anisette Double .... ⎪
Jamaica Shrub..................... ⎭

Spirits per Gallon.

Cognac Brandy ....6*s.* 0*d.*
Hollands ....3*s.* 4*d.*
Jamaica Rum ....5*s.* 0*d.*

MEAT, BREAD, POULTRY, ETC.

	Per lb.
Beef	5d. to 8d.
Mutton	6d. to 8d.
Pork, by the side	5d. to 5½d.
Do., retail,	6d. to 7d.
Do., salted	6d. to 8d.
Bacon	8d. to 9d.
Veal	6d. to 8d.
Lamb	7d. to 8d.
Butter	14d. to 18d.
Bread	1½d. to 2½d.
Eggs, per dozen	8d. to 10d.
Potatoes, per bushel	1s. 3d.
Turkeys	3s. to 7s.
Geese	2s. to 2s. 8d.
Ducks, per couple	2s. 4d. to 3s.
Fowls	2s. 6d. to 4s.
Chickens	2s. 6d. to 3s.
Pigeons	1s. 6d. to 2s. 6d.

N.B. The Guernsey lb. weighs 1½ oz. more than the
English.

Tobacco and Cigars.   Per lb.

Best Turkey	4s.
Common Rag	10d.
Best Real Havannah Cigars, per hundred	10s.
Cubas	do. 8s.
Dutch	do. 2s. 6d.

Snuff.   Per lb.

Real Bolangaro	4s.
Real Strasburg	4s.

Per lb.

Princessa .... : .... , ... 2*s.*
Welsh.... .... 3*s.*
Rappee ....1*s.* 2*d.*

Groceries, &c.

Moist Sugars ....4*d.* to 6*d.*
Lump or Loaf ....5½*d.* to 7*d.*
Souchong Teas....... ....3*s.* to 5*s.*
Green   do. ....; 5*s.* to 7*s.*
Gunpowder do.......... ....7*s.* to 8*s.*
Coffee...... ....1*s.* to 1*s.* 2*d.*
Tapioca ....6*d.*
Rice...... ....4*d.* and 4½*d.*
Arrow Root ....1*s.* 6*d.*
Zante Currants ....8*d.*
English Starch.. ....10*d.*
French   do. ....6*d.*

Soap and Candles.

Yellow Soap ....4*d.* to 6*d.*
Windsor do...... ....1*s.* 2*d.*
Wax Candles....... ... .2*s* 6*d.*
Moulds.. ....8*d.*
Kensington.... ....9*d.*
Rush Candles . , ...6½*d.*
Dips . , ... ,, , ... ,, ..6½*d.* to 7*d.*

CHAPTER XI.

FOR a knowledge of the geology of Guernsey, we are indebted to the late Dr. Macculloch, Vice-President of the Royal Geological Society, a native of. the island, and one of its brightest ornaments, well known as the author of many learned and valuable works on various subjects.

The island of Guernsey is almost entirely of granite formation. The southern division consists entirely of gneiss, and the rocks which form the northern part exhibit various kinds of granite, or granitel. The rock on which Castle Cornet is built, is a gneiss, often approaching so near to granite, as to render its place in a nomenclature doubtful. It is every where crossed and inter-sected by veins of quartz, of trap, and of felspar, curved and mixed in various ways, but tending on the whole to the north or north-east. More early there were found in it veins of brick, red and bright green felspar; and pebbles of the same substance, or with hornblende imbedded, are found on the beach, as well as coarse agates passing into quartz and hornstone.

Proceeding from the castle southwards, gneiss is found to constitute the cliffs on the eastern side, often in a state of decomposition, and covered with a great depth of debris. These strata, which extend all along the south coast to Rocquaire Bay, seem to tend from north-east to south-west, and

o

having various inclinations, but most generally ten or fifteen degrees dipping to the south. On the southern side of the island they are intersected by veins of white, flesh-coloured, and red felspar, of various breadths. In some places the felspar veins pass into granite; veins of quartz and veins of granitel, consisting of quartz and felspar, also traverse it. A few veins of trap are also found intersecting it at Rocquaine, which are occasionally superseded by trap, porphyry, or by the same substance containing minute grains of quartz. In this track there are wrought three or four quarries of black granitel, consisting of hornblende and quartz, and very hard.

A ledge of rocks, called the Hanois, extends from the westernmost point of the island, and from its apparent geographical continuity is probably of the same structure. Against this point the whole strength of the western ocean is directed, and it is from hence that a large ridge of rounder masses of stone has been rolled, so as to form a natural barrier near Rocquaine.

In quitting the elevated parts of the island, and with it the southern shores, the gneiss disappears, and its place is supplied by other granitic formations. Besides the trap and trap porphyry at Rocquaine, there are masses of micaceous schist, having the appearance of veins; and a stratum of argillaceous schist may also be observed at the lower parts of the bay, incumbent on the granitic foundation.

At Le Rée and Lihou, the rocks are composed of quartz and felspar, the foliated textures having disappeared. A granitel is thus formed, which, in some places receiving an addition of hornblende, passes into sienite; this is traversed here and there by veins of the same red and green felspar which are found at Castle Cornet. The same highly-coloured felspars are also occasionally intermixed, so as to form a constituent part of the granite, which thus becomes exceedingly beautiful.

At Grand Rocque are masses of sienite, which are quarried to make building stones. It is the only rock of this nature in the island, and its produce is fully equal in beauty to that of the celebrated quarries of Mont Mado, in Jersey, although it cannot be raised in such large masses.

The predominant rock towards the bay of St. Sampson's is a grey or black granitel, consisting of quartz and hornblende mixed in various proportions. Detached masses of this rock are also found in the higher grounds, as well as among the gneiss of the southern coast. The hornblende in some places predominates, so as to give a sort of hornblende porphyry, and in others every other ingredient is excluded, and a hornblende rock alone remains.

It is remarkable that there is no appearance of limestone in the island.

CONCHOLOGY.

On the Shells, Corals, and Sea Plants of the Channel Islands.

Perhaps there is no portion of the globe of the same extent that can vie with these islands in

conchological treasures; where so many striking
studies of shells are afforded, or where a greater
variety of testaceous and crustaceous subjects
can be collected. The divisions of the order
Testacea in these islands extend to upwards of
forty genera, embracing upwards of two hundred
varieties.   Of these the finest specimens are
collected at the island of Herm, but considerable
quantities of shells are found on the beach of St.
Sampson's, Bordeaux, and L'Ancresse Bays; on
market days the fish stalls have generally a good
collection of fresh shells, especially after spring
tides, and every variety may be procured at Mr.
Naftel's, in the Commercial Arcade, who will also
execute any order very skilfully and reasonably.
There are also beautiful fancy articles in shell-work
at this establishment.

The seas of the Channel Islands abound in
sponges. We have little less than forty species
of them, and the corallines, or corals, cannot be
excelled for delicacy and novelty in any part of
the world.

The stranger is strongly recommended to visit
the shell-bank at Herm; the passage across is
very short, and the fare trifling.

CHAPTER XII.

MANUFACTORIES.

GUERNSEY was formerly famous for worsted knit-
stockings, as well as under-garments called Guern-

sey frocks, but this handicraft trade is almost, if
not entirely, lost ; although at both the town and
country hospitals, as well as by many of the peasants, worsted stockings are beautifully knit at
the most reasonable prices, averaging from *ten-
pence* to *fifteen-pence* per pair.

The chief articles of manufacture are those of
tobacco and snuff ; the making of soap and candles, and the Roman cement from the Isle of
Sheppy stones, or from those brought from the
coast of Essex.

There are several extensive brick-kilns, the surplus produce of which is exported to Plymouth,
Portsmouth, Newfoundland, &c.

In the brickfield a mill may be observed, which
is found to grind and prepare the clay for bricks
in a very expeditious and superior manner to the
common spade ; of which a smaller kind is used
at the Hospital for making their dough for bread.
Even in making mortar this mill is used, by which
it is more effectually mixed and better tempered,
saving also a great deal of manual and heavy
labour.

In 1827, a paper manufactory was established
at Petit Bo Bay. There are also large manufactories for ropes, cordage, twines, for shipping ;
and manufactories of chocolate, cocoa, quinine
bark ; of Glauber and Epsom salts, for the London
and Bristol markets.

Distilleries.

Cider is made in large quantities, and vinegar
also for exportation.

There are distilleries for extracting spirits from potatoes, the exports from which average 24,000 gallons per annum.

The cultivation of the potato forms one of the principal branches of local trade, the exportation of which increases yearly,

In 1833-4	....	92,296 bushels.
1836-7	....	217,303 ..
1839-40	....	376,160 ..

which shews that the culture of this valuable root is found extremely profitable; for, assuming the price last year to have averaged 14*d.* per bushel, which is a low figure, we shall have a sum-total of 21,942*l.* for potatoes exported, divided amongst our farmers, one-third of which, or 7,314*l.*, may be reckoned as clear profit, after the rent of the land and all expense of culture paid.

We have also a manufactory for fine liqueurs, in imitation of the West India cordials.

Native Artists.

Nor are we behind the rest of the world in the fine arts, as many fine paintings testify, from the pencil of the late Mr. Young. We have several native artists:—Le Page, Tosdevin, De Garis, and Naftel's beautiful sketches and masterly style, would take a high stand amongst England's best artists.

LOCAL INSTITUTIONS.

The Mechanics' Institution, States' Arcade, which consists of upwards of four hundred mem-hers, and its library contains more than 3,000 volumes. This library is open every day (Sundays excepted) from eleven in the forenoon to three in the afternoon, and from six to nine in the evening.

Terms of admission:—Members, 12s.; Ladies and Junior Members, 6s. per annum.

Guernsey Choral and Instrumental Society.
Number of Members, 120.
Subscribers, 15s. per annum.

Bible Societies.
British and Foreign Bible Society.
Guernsey Auxiliary to the Trinitarian Bible Society.
Ladies' Association ditto.

Missionary Societies.
Church Missionary Society.
Society for the Propagation of the Gospel in Foreign Parts.
Wesleyan Missionary Society.
London   ditto   Independents.
Methodist New Connexion.
Moravian   ditto.
Primitive Methodist New Connexion.
Bible Christian   ditto.
Baptist   ditto.

Miscellaneous.
Provident Society.
Society for the Promotion of Christianity among the Jews.
Church Pastoral Aid Society.

Irish Society.
Société Evangelique.
Irish Scripture Reader.
Christian Knowledge Society.
Bethel Union.
Ami des Pauvres.
Humane Society.
Benevolent or Strangers' Friend Society.
Charitable Association.
Guernsey Agricultural Society.
Guernsey Horticultural Society.
Temperance Society.
Society for Promoting Industry.
Mutual Insurance Society.

Schools.

Miss Hayes, Saumarez-street.
Misses Mills, Vauvert-road.
Miss Cross, New-street.
Miss Walsh, St. James-street.
Miss Marrett, Mill-street.
Mr. Hayes, Saumarez-street.
Mr. Percy, Clifton.
Miss Barry, Berthelot-street.
Misses Le Ber, Berthelot-street.
Berthelot-street Infant School.
St. John's Infant School, Amballes.
British and Foreign School, established Jan. 4, 1843,
    New Place, Vauvert road.

There are no less than thirteen Sunday and other schools in the Town parish only, with a total of 2,242 scholars, of whom 1,257 are educated by the Church of England.

READING ROOMS.

The Independent Club Room,

next to Marshall's Hotel, is the oldest establishment, well supplied with newspapers and news of all kinds, whether *local* or foreign, and is the usual resort of the Island gentlemen, but from this strangers are excluded.

Redstone's Reading Room and Circulating Library,

in the Commercial Arcade, is open to strangers and visitors every day from eight o'clock, A. M., in summer, and nine o'clock, A. M., in winter, closing at nine in the evening. This establishment is lighted with gas and supplied with the best newspapers of England, Guernsey, and Jersey, and the most interesting periodicals of the day. The terms for residents are, for the year, £2; for 6 months, 1*l*. 8*s*.; for 3 months, 16*s*. 6*d*.; for 6 weeks, 10*s*.; 4 weeks, 8*s*.; 2 weeks, 4*s*. 6*d*.; 1 week, 2*s*. 6*d*. The circulating Library contains all modern standard works. Since the first edition of this Guide, a new establishment has been formed.

The Civil and United Service Club,

offers a splendid saloon, 51 feet long, handsomely furnished, lighted with gas, and having also Billiard, Card, and Refreshment Rooms. It is *open to strangers* and visitors, by introduction of members, for one month; after which period they may become Quarterly Subscribers during their stay in the Island, or for any length of time they please. Resident members must be annual subscribers. The Reading Room is supplied with London and local newspapers, periodicals, &c. (The Lieut.-Governor and Bailiff of the Island are honorary members, as also the officers of the garrison). The subscription is three pounds per annum, with one pound entrance. Strangers one pound quarterly.

THE PUBLIC AMUSEMENTS.

Races

take place annually in June, when a royal cup, for the improvement of the Island breed of horses, is granted by her Majesty. Also a government plate, with several handicaps and sweepstakes prizes by subscription are offered for competition, open to all horses.

Regatta.

In 1841, a cup value 100 guineas was offered to the Yacht Clubs of the United Kingdom. In 1842, it was sailed for by six yachts, eleven leagues over a well-chosen course in sight of the town, and was won by the Union of Cork, — Morris, Esq., after a beautiful and well-contested race. Prizes for sailing and row-boats were also contested by pilots and amateurs.

Fishing

from boats and from the rocks in the various delightful bays is very good. In summer, a variety of fish is taken by the hook, seines, and trawls. A sporting club of gentlemen frequent the northern coast for this amusement and convivial meetings.

Hunting.

There is no established pack of hounds in the Island from the paucity of hares. There are a few couples of harriers supported by amateurs, and game is imported from France and England for the chase.

Cricket.

The clubs of Guernsey and Jersey meet in the summer: and matches and weekly meetings take place in the new ground, where some good play may be seen.

Assembly Rooms.

The winter balls are open to the army and navy. Strangers require an introduction for admittance. The rooms are spacious, well-lighted, and convenient: the price of tickets moderate.

With a good introduction, there are few places where the lovers of gaiety can find better amusement than in this little Island. The society is select and pleasant. Picnics and evening dances are constantly going on; and in the summer both are combined about once a fortnight; when country parties are formed at a very moderate expense, and rendezvous made at some beautiful part of the Island.

ENGLISH SERVICES IN THE VARIOUS PLACES OF
WORSHIP IN THE TOWN.

EPISCOPALIAN.

Parochial Church.—Garrison Service, at half-
past 12, on Sundays.   Minister: Rev. W. Le
Mottée.

St. James's Church.—On Sundays, at half-past
10 in the forenoon, and half-past 6 in the evening.
Wednesdays, at half-past 6 in the evening.   Minister: Rev. J. Hawtrey.

St. John's Church.—On Sundays, at the same
hours as at *St. James's.*   Thursdays, at half-past
6 in the evening.   Minister: Rev. E. G. Carr.

Bethel Chapel, Manor-street.—On Sundays, at
half-past 10 in the forenoon, and at half-past 6 in
the evening.   Minister: Rev. A. T. Corfe.

St. Peter-Port Sunday School.—On Sundays,
at 10 in the forenoon, and at half-past 6 in the
evening.   Minister: Rev. C. C. Mulloy.

WESLEYAN.

Ebenezer Chapel, New Town.—On Sundays, at
half-past 10 in the forenoon, and at 6 in the
evening.   On Wednesdays and Fridays, at 7 in
the evening.   Ministers: Revs. G. Jackson and
W. Etheridge.

Wesley Chapel, Bouët.—On Sundays, at half-
past 2 in the afternoon.   Mondays at 7 in the
evening.

INDEPENDENT.

Eldad Chapel, New Town.—On Sundays, at

half-past 10 in the forenoon; at 3 in the afternoon, and at half-past six in the evening. Mondays and Thursdays, at 7 in the evening. Minister: Rev. W. Wild.

METHODIST NEW CONNEXION.

Zion Chapel, Clifton.—On Sundays, at half-past 10 in the forenoon, and at 6 in the evening. Wednesdays and Fridays, at 7 in the evening. Present Minister: Rev. — Beansley.

BIBLE CHRISTIANS.

Salem Chapel, Vauvert-road.—On Sundays, at half-past 10 in the forenoon, and at 6 in the evening. Tuesdays and Thursdays, at 7 in the evening. Present Minister: Rev. R. Tabb.

PRIMITIVE METHODISTS.

Primitive Methodist Chapel, Truchet-street, built in 1841, will contain about 600 persons, is licensed for the celebration of Marriages, and has a Sunday-school connected with it.—Services on Sundays, at half-past 10 in the forenoon, and 6 in the evening. On Tuesdays, at 7 in the evening. Minister: Rev. C. Jones.

BAPTIST CHAPEL.

Baptist Chapel in Wesley Road, built in 1840, will accommodate 280 persons.—There are two public services on the Sabbath, commencing at half-past 10 in the forenoon, and 6 in the evening. Prayer-meeting on Monday evening at 7 o'clock,

P

and on Thursday evening a Lecture at the same hour. Minister: Rev. T. Spurgeon.

BAPTIST CHAPEL.

At Tower-Hill, opened for public Worship by the Rev. J. Burroughes.—On Sunday, at half-past 10 in the forenoon, and 6 in the evening. Also on Wednesday, at 7 in the evening.

FRIENDS.

Meeting-House, Clifton.—On Sundays, at 10 in the forenoon, and at 3 in the afternoon. Thursdays, at 10 in the forenoon.

ROMAN CATHOLIC.

Burnt-Lane Chapel.—On Sundays, at 8 and 11 o'clock in the forenoon, and at 3 o'clock in the afternoon. Minister: Rev. J. Connaty.

BETHEL UNION.

Preaching-Room, on the Quays.—On Sundays, at half-past 10 in the forenoon, at half-past 2 in the afternoon, and at 6 in the evening. Thursdays, at 7 in the evening. Ministers: Various.

PLYMOUTH BRETHREN.

Preaching-Room, Berthelot-street. — On Sundays, at half-past 10 in the forenoon, at half-past 2 in the afternoon, and at half-past 6 in the evening. Tuesdays and Fridays, at 7 in the evening. Minister: Rev. H. De St. Dalmas.

LOCAL NEWSPAPERS.

The Star—published on Monday and Thursday.

The Comet—Mondays and Thursdays.

La Gazette de Guernsey—a paper chiefly of advertisements—Saturday.

Church of England Magazine (in French).

Wesleyan Magazine　　　　　　(do.)

New Connexion Methodist Magazine (do.)

LAWS RELATIVE TO SPORTING.

On the numerous complaints of the inhabitants of the country parishes of the great injury caused to them by persons shooting, who, though armed with guns, make use of ferrets, and, accompanied sometimes by ten or twelve dogs, devastate the fields and gardens, break down hedges, fire into orchards, kill poultry, frighten cattle, and even alarm people in their houses,—The court, specially assembled on this subject, considering the great change which has taken place in the face of the country since the various ordinances relating to sporting were emanated,—that there are now neither hares, pheasants, nor partridges,—that the number of furze fields and other uncultivated grounds has vastly diminished, and that the only game, with the exception of a few rabbits, is reduced to the woodcock, snipe, and other migratory birds; considering, above all, the necessity of protecting the inhabitants in their

houses and out-premises, and of repressing the
offences which are committed by fines more ade-
quate than those hitherto imposed,—The court,
after taking hereon the conclusions of the crown
officers, has ordered, and doth hereby order, that
all preceding ordinances relating to sporting, and
to dogs, shall be annulled, and that the following
regulations shall be substituted therefor:—

1. All persons, except such as have a right of warren,
are prohibited from keeping or having ferrets in their
possession. And such as have a right of warren are
forbidden to use their ferrets elsewhere than in their
warrens, or on lands belonging to them; and they are
also forbidden to lend their ferrets for the purpose of
their being used elsewhere than on their own warrens or
lands, or on the lands of the persons to whom the ferrets may be lent. The whole on pain of a fine, which,
at the discretion of the court, and according to the
exigency of the case, both on the person lending the
ferrets and on the person to whom they shall have been
lent, shall not exceed 20l. sterling on each.

2. All persons are prohibited from going through the
country parts of the ten parishes of this island, even
without a gun, with more than three dogs,—or, having
a gun, with more than two dogs. and this, whether in
either case there be two or more persons in company,—
the whole under pain of a fine not exceeding 20l. sterling for each person.

3. All minors under sixteen years of age are forbidden
to go sporting with any description of gun, on pain of
a fine, at the discretion of the court, which shall not
exceed 20l.

4. Every stranger not paying rates, (officers in garrison bearing his Majesty's commission excepted), is for-

bidden to go sporting, or to go about the country with a
gun, unless he be accompanied by an inhabitant paying
rates, who shall be responsible for the damage that may
be caused by the said stranger, and also for the payment
of all the fines he may incur; on pain of a fine, at the
discretion of the court, not exceeding 20*l.* sterling.

5. All persons are prohibited from entering orchards
with a gun, and from going, either with a gun or with
dogs, into granaries, yards, or gardens attached to farm-
houses, on pain of a fine, at the discretion of the court,
which shall not exceed 10*l.* sterling, in all cases where
no gun shall have been fired in the said places, nor 20*l.*
sterling in cases where a gun may have been fired.
And the proprietor of such orchards, &c., shall be a
competent witness in all cases where he is alone, provided he abandon his share of the fine in favour of the
poor.

6. All persons are prohibited from sporting on any
cultivated lands or meadows from the 1st March to the
1st October, unless it be on their own land, or on other
land with the permission of the proprietor, on pain of a
fine, at the discretion of the court, which shall not exceed 20*l.* sterling.

7. It is forbidden to go sporting in any manner on
the Sunday, either with gun or with dog, on pain of a
fine, at the discretion of the court, not exceeding 20*l.*
And the fact of having fired a gun, though but once,
will be deemed sufficient proof that the person was
sporting.

8. It is forbidden to set snares, gins, or nets on the
premises of another person, with a view to take rabbits
or other game, without the permission of the proprietor
of the land, on pain of a fine, at the discretion of the
court, not exceeding 20*l.* sterling.

9. All persons keeping dogs are forbidden to allow

them to go about without a collar bearing the owner's name, excepting when they are out sporting, on pain of a fine, at the discretion of the court, not exceeding 5*l.* sterling. And every dog found about the country without such collar, and without master, or other person claiming him, shall be liable to be killed on the order of any constable so finding him.

10. Considering the injury frequently caused to sheep by dogs, and the peculiarity of the case, every honest man will be credited upon his oath, or any other person of good character for him, as to the injury which may have been caused to his sheep by any dog or dogs, in his presence, or in that of any other witness.

11. In the event of its being proved by two witnesses that a dog shall have worried, killed, or otherwise destroyed any sheep, it shall be presumed that all the sheep worried or killed in the same parish within the preceding fortnight, have been so worried or killed by the same dog, and the owner of it shall be bound to pay the value of the sheep so worried or killed: provided, however, that the amount of the loss shall have been properly ascertained, and that it shall have been reported to one of the constables of the parish within twenty-four hours after it shall have taken place.

12. In the event of a dog being seen attacking sheep, but without either killing or visibly worrying them, the owner of such dog shall be liable to a fine, which, at the discretion of the court, shall not exceed 10*l.* sterling.

And the fines shall be applied—one-fourth to the king, one-fourth to the poor, and one-half to the informer.

And this present ordinance shall be published, &c.

GOVERNMENT POST OFFICE, &c.

Captain Fell, Postmaster, Arcade. Le Mesurier, Assistant Postmaster. The office is open every day in the week, from seven o'clock in the morning until eight in the evening, from the 5th March to the 5th November; and from eight to eight, from the 5th November to the 5th March. On Sundays, the office closes at two o'clock, P. M. The packets arrive every Sunday and Thursday from Weymouth.

New Regulations.—When her Majesty's packets leave Jersey or Guernsey at, or before, 4 o'clock in the morning, in Summer, and 5 in the Winter, the letter-box is closed at 9 o'clock the preceding evening, and a fee of one penny on each letter and newspaper is taken until 10 o'clock, when the mail finally closes. When the packets leave Jersey after 4 o'clock in Summer, or 5 in Winter, the mail does not close till next morning.

Ship-letter mails, of *paid* or *unpaid* letters, or those bearing the *label stamp* and *stamped covers*, are made up at the General Post-office, to be forwarded by the *private steamers*, provided they are specially directed "*By the private steamers viâ Southampton*," and put into the Post-office *one hour* previous to the time fixed for their departure.

Letter Carriers.

Thomas De La Mare .... Fosse André.

Peter Martin................ Clifton-steps.

Peter Desperques .... Long-store.

John De La Mare .... Pedvin-street.

John Le Messurier .... Fountain-street.

FOREIGN POST-OFFICE.

Matthew Barbet, Postmaster, 23, High-Street; John Barbet, deputy do. The office is open every day in the week (Sunday excepted), from nine in the morning until six in the evening, throughout the year.

Letter Carrier, Peter Desperques, Long-store.

STEAM-PACKET OFFICES.

Atalanta, No. 12, bottom of Fountain-street. Agent: Peter Nicholas Maingy.

Sir Francis Drake, and Commercial Steam-packet Company, No. 23, High-street. Agent: M. Barbet.

Passage Vessels.

Weymouth, Guernsey, and Jersey.—One of Her Majesty's Post-office steam-packets, with the mails and passengers, leaves Weymouth for Guernsey and Jersey every Wednesday and Saturday, at nine o'clock P.M., weather permitting, and leaves the islands for Weymouth every Tuesday and Saturday, the time being dependent on the tide.

	£	s.	d.
Passage-money for cabin passengers to Guernsey	1	1	0
Between Guernsey and Jersey	0	5	0

Southampton, Guernsey, and Jersey. — Two fine steamers run constantly between Southampton and these islands—the days may vary; and in winter they make.but one voyage each during the week; in summer the communication is almost daily. The fares are about the same as from Weymouth.

Plymouth and Guernsey.—The steamer, *Sir Francis Drake*, leaves Plymouth every Thursday evening, arriving in Guernsey every Friday morning, waiting only to land her passengers, and then proceeding to Jersey; she returns the same evening to Plymouth.

	£	s.	d.
Main cabin......................	1	1	0
Fore cabin	0	12	0

Sailing vessels ply between Guernsey and Southampton once a-week. There are two fine cutters fitted up with accommodation for passengers—the *Æolus* and *Princess Charlotte*.

	£	s.	d.
Cabin	0	15	0
Deck	0	7	0

Plymouth and Guernsey.—The cutter *Horatio* every week. Fare 7s.

Brixham and Guernsey.—Two cutters every week, the *Diligence* and *Two Brothers*. Fare 5s.

Guernsey and Jersey.—The cutters *Peggy* and *Mary and Anne* every week. Fare 2s. 6d.

Guernsey and Alderney.—Two fine cutters, the *Experiment* and *Frederick*, once a-week; passage about three hours. Fare 2s. 6d.

Guernsey and Sark.—A great number of boats, with excellent seamen, pass daily to and fro; besides which, two cutters, the *Jane* and the *Mary*, ply regularly every Saturday, and sometimes come in every day. The fare is only 1s.

Guernsey and Cherbourg.—The *Mars* and the *Henry* every week. Fare 10*s.*

Guernsey and St. Malo.—The *Marie Anne* and the *Télémaque* every week. Fare 7*s.* 6*d.*

Passports are given *gratis* at Government House.

Guernsey and Rotterdam.—The schooner *Admiral Wyndham* every month.

Boatmen's Fares.

Boatmen.—Conveyance of passengers from the pier, or from the rocks St. Julien to the roads, or from the roads to the said rock or pier, 10*d.* each passenger, ordinary baggage included.

Conveyance within the pier to or from any vessel, 5*d.* each passenger. No higher demand to be made under a penalty of 14 livres tournois.

Porters.—Carriage of each passenger's effects to the hotels and lodgings at the lower part of the town, 6*d.* under a penalty of 10 livres tournois.

Notice to Mariners.

For the convenience of approaching the roadstead and harbour of the island of Guernsey, a gas light has been erected on the round-house on the south pier head. Its elevation at high-water spring tide is forty feet. This light will be seen coming through the Small Russell from the northward, the Great Russell from the eastward, and also from the southward, when round St. Martin's Point. This round-house serves as a mark for the different channels to the roads by day, and will consequently, from its light, serve by night, as per the following directions:

Vessels coming from the northward and the eastward, through the Great Russell, and bound for the roads or harbour, are to run on to the southward, till they bring the light to bear north-west by north, or open to the southward of Castle Cornet; they may then steer on for the castle, always keeping the light open until within a mile of the said castle, and they will clear the *Têtes d'Aval*, or Lower Heads.

On nearing the castle and running for the harbour, bring the light to bear west-north-west. To anchor in the roads, bring the light to bear west by north—this will be central.

In steering for the Small Russell, bring the Casket lights to bear north-east half north, until you have the pier light bearing south-west by west half west; then steer on for the light, it being the central track for running through that passage.

N. B. — Much caution must be observed by night in running through the Small Russell.

In coming from the southward round St. Martin's point, run to the eastward, until you bring the light to bear north half west; then steer north half east, until you bring it to bear west by north: the light will then be open to the northward of the castle—then run for the roads or harbour.

The light is on the larboard hand going into the harbour, the entrance of which is eighty feet wide.

The above bearings are given by compass.

PHYSICIANS, ETC.

The following list of the physicians and surgeons, amongst whom are some experienced and highly-talented men, may, by its formidable length, impress the stranger with no very favourable opinion of the climate of Guernsey; but he must remember the yet undecided question, of whether "patients make doctors, or doctors make patients." It is only within the last century that the island can boast of more than one M. D. The little island of Sark has never had one *at all* till within the last year; and it is surprising how long-lived and healthy the inhabitants are. The Homœopathic system is about to be practised by Mr. Ozanne, a very talented young man, at present studying in London, who had taken out his diploma as physician in the old system; but has given it up in favour of its antagonist, Homœopathy, which has for some years been privately practised in the island with great success.

Physicians.

S. Elliott Hoskins, F. R. S.
F. P. Hutchinson, Petite Marche.
Francis Scott, Hauteville.
Edward Carey, Hauteville.
De Beauvoir De Lisle, Town Rectory.
Thomas Lukis Mansell, Grange-road.
Frederick C. Lukis, Smith-street.
J. R. M'Cord, Saumarez-street.

Surgeons.

J. T. O'Brien, Smith-street.
John Mauger, Market-street.

N. H. Bisson, Bordage-street.
Gledstanes Carey, Bordage-street.
Nicholas Magrath, under the Arch.
John Roberts, St. James-street.
M. A. B. Corbin, Havilland-street.
N. H. Bisson, jun., Vauvert-road.
P. Tranter, Hauteville.
Robert Goldstone, Rohais.
James Rouillé, Mansell-place.
J. F. Naftel, New Place.
Hugh Monk, Admiralty Surgeon for British Seamen,
    Ann's-place.
W. Mogford, Veterinary Surgeon, Rue Poudreuse, St.
    Martin.

Druggists.

Henry Cumber, Fountain-street.
Henry Gardner, Country Mansell.
Peter Allez, Commercial Arcade.
Adolphus Arnold, do.   do.
Nicholas Mellish and T. P. Naftel, States' Arcade.
W. B. Satterley, Fountain-street.
W. Philpot, Smith-street.

CHRONOLOGICAL EVENTS.

January 21, 1806.—Peter Perchard, Esq., died in Lon-
    don, of which city he was then Lord Mayor.

February 15, 1809.—Colonel Sir George Smith died at
    Cadiz.

March, 9, 1818.—Captain N. Dobree, R. N., drowned,
    with three other natives of the Câtel parish, in

Q

attempting to save the crew of a foreign vessel wrecked in Cobo Bay.

March 15, 1837.—Colonel Oliver de Lancey, of the British Auxiliary Legion in Spain, and late Captain of the 60th or King's Rifles, mortally wounded near St. Sebastian, and died the 22nd.

April 14, 1821.—Sir Peter de Havilland, Bailiff, died in Guernsey, aged 73.

April 17, 1830.—Colonel W. de Vic Tupper killed in Chili, aged 29.

„ 24, 1794.—Lieutenant Carré Tupper, H. M. S. Victory, only son of Major-General Tupper, killed near Bastia.

May 5, 1836.—Captain John Alles, of the British Auxiliary Legion in Spain, killed near St. Sebastian.

„ Colonel William Le Mesurier Tupper, of the British Auxiliary Legion in Spain, and late Captain of the 23rd, or Royal Welsh Fusileers, mortally wounded near St. Sebastian, and died the 13th, aged 32.

June 18, 1826.—Lieutenant E. W. Tupper, H. M. S. Sybille, mortally wounded near Candia, and died at Malta the 26th.

July 22, 1822.—Major General Le Marchant, aged 47, and Lieutenant-Colonel Barlow, killed, and Ensign H. Le Mesurier lost his right arm, at the battle of Salamanca.

June 21, 1809.—Captain Rawdon M'Crea and Ensign Le Serre, 87th Regiment, killed at Talavera.

June — — Colonel Havilland Le Mesurier killed at the battle of the Pyrenees.

August 21, 1835.—Doctor John Macculloch died. The Author of " Proof and Illustrations of the Attributes of God, from the Facts and Laws of the Physical Universe," &c., " The Islands and Western Isles of Scotland," " A System of Geology," and many other valuable and learned works. Dr. Macculloch was fellow of the Royal, the Linnæan, and Geological Societies, and at one time Vice-President of the last. He was also Physician in Ordinary to Prince Leopold of Saxe Coburg.

  " —, 1825.—Peter Paul Dobree, an eminent Classical Scholar, who at the time of his early death, was Regius Professor of Greek at the University of Cambridge, and deeply lamented as one in whom Greek Literature had sustained a heavy loss. He was the learned author of " Porsoni Aristophanes," " Adversaria," " Lexicon Rhetoricum Cantabrigiense," &c., &c. With Dr. Macculloch he deserves to be remembered as one of the brightest ornaments of his native Island.

September —, 1842.—Daniel de Lisle Brock, the late Bailiff of Guernsey, died. He filled that high office with faithfulness and zeal, and a public funeral was unanimously decreed as a slight testimony to his upright discharge of every public duty during forty-three years.

October 9, 1836.—Admiral the Right Honourable Lord De Saumarez, K.C.B., K. S., &c., &c., &c., died, aged 79.

October 13, 1812.—Major-General Sir Isaac Brock, K. B., slain in Canada. Two of his brothers, Lieutenant-Colonel John Brock, and Lieutenant Ferdinand Brock, were both killed in the army before him.

,, 14, 1747.—Captain Philip de Saumarez, H.M.S. Nottingham, killed in action.

November 19, 1800.—Nicholas Dobree, Esq., of Belle Vue, in this island, died, aged 68. The regiment of Militia Artillery, which he commanded, was first raised and organized by him.

,, ,, 1800.—William Le Marchant died. He was Bailiff of the island thirty years, and filled that situation with such fidelity and ability, that the decisions pronounced under his administration rank as the soundest upon record.

,, ,, 1840.—Peter Martin Carey died. He spent the greater part of his life out of his native island; yet contributed largely towards the De La Cour Fund for the relief of such distressed native mariners and fishermen as should be cast destitute on the coast; and his influence was ever thrown in on behalf of Guernsey rights, laws, and liberties.

December ,, 1813.—Lieutenant P. Le Mesurier, of the 9th Regiment, killed in Spain.

,, ,, 1813.—Captain Carey Le Marchant, of the 1st Foot Guards, eldest son of the before-mentioned Major-General Le Marchant, mortally wounded in Spain.

,, ,, 1840.—Lieutenant Bulkeley George Le Mesurier, H.M.S. Talbot, killed at the bombardment of Acre.

173

CHAPTER XIII.

GUERNSEY FRENCH.

THE language of the townspeople, from their constant intercourse with strangers, is very intelligible English, though spoken with a peculiar accent, and frequently interlarded with the mother-tongue; but in the country, or if marketing on a Saturday, when the town is thronged with peasants, the stranger may be greatly puzzled to make out what language the people are talking. It is a good old dialect, which, during the last century at least, has proceeded in a steady course of gathering, like a rolling snowball, from every thing it encountered, and increasing its vocabulary by various compounds of Latin, Welsh, Scotch, German, English, Italian, added to the original stock, which was Norman-French, making altogether a very expressive, and by no means an unharmonious patois.

If it *seems* to be rude and harsh, it is because you do not hear it kindly spoken; because perhaps you listen to the contentions of the market-place, or the coarse voices on the pier,—no language is euphonious in these places. You must go to the fireside and hear a kind mother speaking to her child, "*Mon p' tit canard de soué,*" "*Ma poulette.*" Hear the young girl tell of her heart's love, or ask her to sing you a song, "*Dans le*

Q 3

forêt du bouais d'amour," or *" Belle rose au rosier bllian ;"* or,

> *" Chètait par un dimanch au ser,*
> *" Au biau kler de la lune."*

Then get an old woman to tell you stories of her young life, *" Le bouan vier tems,"* and then judge of our Guernesiais.

As to *expression*, I defy any language to express the hot impatience of a hungry man better than by *" Hurle mé un gobbin de chet houichepott là,"* which means "Throw me a piece of that pudding;" yet how tame is the translation!

Of single words, I know none in any language more comprehensive than the following:

Un bad' la goule	A chatter-box
La bedi bédoue	Stomach-ache
Cod pouagnair	To thump
Chafernaeux	Squeamish, particular
Guerlair	To squall
Eperki	To perch
Etchippair	To throw
Equagahie	Stiff-bruised
Declaqinair	To hurry off
Derocquair	To fall down
Dedjougllial	Out of order

These are but a few of their single *emphatics;* but often they take up an English word, and use it as one of their own in the oddest way imaginable. You may hear one say to another, as they pass up and down Smith-street on a windy day, *" I vente un fier breeze agniet au yous"*—"It blows a fine breeze to-day." The *" au yous,"* or *" au tu,"* is merely an expletive, and is equivalent to "say then," or "I say."

I remember once hearing of a woman, who, in describing an apology made to her by some offending neighbour, said, "*A' vint en flag'atruce me le dire*"—the English "flag of truce" was made to serve her purpose well.

Another time, two fat persons were driving on the Esplanade in a gig, with a little boy most miserably stuck in between them, and a country woman, as they passed, exclaimed "*Ah mais v'la donc un poore éfant drollement posturais.*" The words "poor" and "posture" were thus frenchified in this sentence.

But not to make this chapter too long, I will now only give the stranger a few Guernsey phrases and words which he will find most useful, if he wishes to make himself "at home" with our good Guernsey folk, or if he wishes to understand their politeness, their kindness, their fun, for they have plenty of all these in their own way. I will also, where I *can*, give the probable derivation of the words, as well as the French and English.

GUERNSEY PHRASES.

Guernesiais.	*French.*	*English.*
Frume l'usse	Fermez la porte	Shut the door
V'nai cant é mé	Venez avec moi	Come with me
Kique tu fais îlot	Que fais-tu là	What are you doing
Remouque té / Avanche donc }	Depêche-toi	Make haste
Vi t'en agniet	Viens aujourd'hui	Come to-day
Amarre mé chunna	Attache-moi cela	Tie this for me
Au couain du faeu	Auprès du feu	By the fire-side
Tais ta goule	Taisez-vous	Hold your tongue
Au ras de mé	Auprès de moi	Close to me
J'sie hardi enrimai	J'ai une rhume	I have a bad cold
Echippe mè chunna	Jette-moi cela	Throw me that
J'sie enverrai		I am teased
Ne me fai donc pouint étrivain }		Don't provoke me
Ah'que t'es geurgi pountant }		How cross you are
Ché nott lavin agniet		It is our washing day

Guernesiais.	French.	English.
Accluiquie		Sitting all of a heap
Aigue	Aide	Help
Aiguchier l'bec	Se faire un appetit	To get an appetite
Agniet	Aujourd'hui	To-day
Accouaint		Acquaintance
Akatair	Acheter	To buy
Arlevaie	L'après-midi	Afternoon
Angliaitin	Anglais(par mépris)	English
Abimair	Gronder fortement	To scold
Atre ᵃ	Foyer	Hearth
Bragi	Ivre	Drunk
Braies ᵇ	Culottes	Breeches
Banatrês		Lobster pots
Bliase	Brune	Fog
Baheur	Coffre	Trunk
Bêlle	Cour d'une maison	Court yard
Bingue	Panier	Basket
Baué ᶜ	Boue	Mud
Bad'lagoule ᵈ		Chatter-box
Brioche	Couteau à chasse	Clasp knife
{ Boucas		Rubbish
{ Ramasse ton boucas }		Gather up your rubbish
Bouket	Seau	Bucket
{ Boucaillière	Houspiller	Worry
{ Badrin		To bother
{ Che badrin		What a botheration
Baguiare	Cerises	Small cherries
Baillot	Cure	Wash-tub
{ Crasset ᵉ	Lampe	A cresset lamp
{ Crastillair	Etinceller	To sparkle
Courtil	Champ	Field
Crabe-a-col	Ecrevisse de mer	Cray-fish

ᵃ *Atre*, perhaps from the Latin *ara*—the altar on the hearth to the household god.

ᵇ *Braies*, no doubt from *brackeæ*—breeches.

ᶜ *Baué*, possibly from *baw* (Welsh).

ᵈ *Bad'lagoule*, from *balugola* (Italian).

ᵉ *Crasset* is very likely derived from cresset, a light suspended; in all the country cottages they have, hanging, oil-lamps just over the table in summer, or depending from the chimney-piece in winter. Milton and Shakespear both use this word. See *Paradise Lost*, b. i. 726:

> " from the arched roof,
> Pendent by subtle magic, many a row
> Of starry lamps and blazing cressets.

And Shakespear, in *1st Henry IV.*, act 3. *Glendower* speaks,—
> " at my nativity
> The front of heaven was full of fiery shapes,
> Of burning cressets."

Guernesiais.	French.	English.
Caûches[f]	Bas	Stockings
Chunna	Cela	That
Courtine	Rideau	Curtain
Coue[g]	Queue	Tail
Chtinchin	Celui-ci	This one
Couayair	Epargner	To spare
Devallair	Descendre	To descend
Debranki	Salope	Slovenly
Devanté	Tablier	Apron
Douit[h]	Ruisseau	Brook
D'vis	Entretien	Conversation
Doublièr	Nappe	Tablecloth
Démarrai	Detacher	To untie
Désaquiair	Decamper	To decamp
Drissair	Glisser	To slide
Drêchair	Servir le dîner	To dish up
Dolaeures	Copeaux	Shavings
Destorbair	Deranger	To disturb
Epille	Epingle	Pin
Effan	Enfant	Child
Etrivair	Agacer	To tease
Etrain	Paille	Straw
Eloquiair[i]	Secouer	To shake
Enfrouagnie[k]	Ridé	Wrinkled
Ecarse	Rare	Rare, scarce
Econfiliair	Amenuseir	To chip
Filie		Limpet
Fairè la vie[l]	Gronder	To scold
Fikis	Fixer	To fix
Les fins faeux[m]		At full speed
Guergi	Grogner	Cross
Gabarrair		To skull a boat
Gradille	Groseille à grappe	Currants
Groir	s'habiller	To dress

[f] *Caûches*, perhaps from *cothurnus*, a sock or boot worn by tragedians.

[g] *Coue*, from *cauda* (Latin), a tail.

[h] *Douit*, in Angevin, is a brook; from the Gaulish *dwy*, the same, or simply water.

[i] *Eloquiair* and *eloquant*, to shake, from *locha, loka,* Armorican, whence *lochar,* Guerns., to shake or rock.

[k] *Enfrouagnie*, or *enferouagni*, from the same; English, *frown;* and French, *froncer,* which are both derived from the Celtic *frên,* or *brôn.*

[l] *Fairè la vie* is an ellipsis of " Faire la vie du diable," make a row.

[m] *Les fins faeux; fins* means extreme; *faeux,* the plu. of *feu,* fire,—possibly alluding to the swiftness of the running fire of the Prairies.

Guernesiais.	French.	English.
Garce	Fille	Girl
Gaûche	Gâteau	Cake
Guervai	Faché	Vexed
Gilliannair	Cueillir	To gather flowers
Gorbon ᵃ		Peat
Grimair	Egratigner	To scratch
Houlair	Jeter	To throw
Haistair	Hisser	To hoist
Houichba ᵇ		
Houichepotte	Poudin	Pudding
Haentair	Frequenter	{ To associate with, to haunt
Hardi	Beaucoup	A great deal
Hayemie ᵈ	La haye du milieu	The middle hedge
Iragne ᶠ	Araignée	Spider
Ichin	Ici	Here
Jonquière ᵍ		
Jaonniere	{ Champ de genet epineux }	Furze field
Kerru ᵗ	Gaillard	Hearty
Kerbon	Charbon	Coal
Kerrue	Charrue	Plough
Kerouin	Vaurien	Rascal

ᵃ *Gorbon*, from *corban*, a gift, so called at its discovery in Vaxon Bay.

ᵇ *Houichba*, going out in the snow when the birds are tamed by the cold, and knocking them down, or catching them on their perch at night, with a lantern.

ᵈ *Houichepotte.* I find no connexion between this word and any language I know of, unless it be the English *wish-pot*, in times when pudding was a greater treat than it is in these days.

ᵈ *Hayemie*, the middle hedge, *haga media*, of base latinity.

ᶠ *Iragne, airagne*, old French; *ragna*, Italian.

ᵍ *Jonquière*, the square bed frame, about a foot and a half high, which is placed in every Guernsey cottage near the fire, covered with dried fern or pease-straw, where the old women knit, and the girls sing, flirt, &c. &c., summer and winter. It is also called *lit de vielle*, and *lit de faille* ᵉ.

> ᵉ Un ser, j'etais dans ma cabutte,
>   Assis au couain d'une belle fouaie d'vrec,
> De bouan cidre dan ma jutte,
>   Et le p'tit but d'pipe au man bec:
> L'vent qui hurlait dans ma guerbière
> Faisait que l'crasset brûlait blleu,
> Ma femme ouvrait su la jonquière.
>   *   *   *   *
>   *La vielle Marie.*

ᵗ *Kerru* also means "piquante," a relish, *J'me faut de ké kerru.*

Guernesiais.	French.	English.
Keure	Querir	To fetch
Lures	Historiettes	Tales
Lliotin		Small whiting
Lakair	Laisser	To leave
Liaire	Lire	To read
{ Lavresse*	Blanchisseuse	A washerwoman
{ Lavin	Blanchissage	The wash
{ Lavechin ˣ		Little wash
Marri	Douleur, chagrin	Anger, grief
Minchair	Casser	To break
Muisson	Oiseau	A bird
Minotte	Petite main	Small hand
Mourionnair		To move quick
Mâquair		To chew
Nouairʸ	Nager	To swim
Nouches	Mariage	Wedding
Niet	Nuit	Night
Niais ˢ		Foolish
Niòllin	Galimatias	Nonsense
{ Ouvrai }	Tricoter	To knit
{ Ouvrettai }		
Ozanne	Carreau de vitre	A pane of glass
Orkière	Ornière	Wheel rut
Paretᵃ	Paroi	Wall
Pâtenotesᵇ	Perles	Beads
Patouaillair	Patiner	To paw
Pingueux	Aiguittier	Needle-case
Pernaguiair	Faire des cabrioles	To cut capers
Palfrandingue		{ An expression of sur-prise or anger
Ramader	Raccomoder	To mend
Rouanairᵉ	Gronder	To scold
Ragotter	Frapper	To beat
R'virair	Retourner	To return
R'nêchonnairᵈ		
R'nouvé	Le printemps	Spring

ˢ *Lavin* and *Lavresse*, from *lavo*, to wash.

ˣ *Lavechin*, a little wash; they make their diminutives like the Germans with *chen*, *chin*.

ʸ *Nouair*; Italian, *nuotare*, to swim.

ˢ *Niais* and *niau*, from oiseau *niais*, literally *nideus*, or *nidasius*, a nestling bird, a fool.

ᵃ *Paret*, from *Paries*, *parietis*, Latin, whence the French *paroi*.

ᵇ *Pâtenotes*, from *Pater-noster*, the rosary.

ᵉ *Rouanair* seems to be derived from the old English word *round*, or *rowne*, to mutter, to grumble.

ᵈ *R'nêchonnair*, a Guernsey custom, that the bride and bride-groom go to church almost in a marriage procession the Sunday after their wedding.

Guernesiais.	French.	English.
Soulair [a]	Avoir coûtume	To be accustomed
{ Soudardire { Soudarderie [f] } Soldatesque		Belonging to soldiers
Souventre	Suivre	To go after a person
Tracas	Sottise	Stuff, nonsense
Terpi [g]	Trepied	A tripod
Troubllair	Enrager	A mad person
Terrien	Laboreur	A labourer
Tchufouarait		A term of reproach
Us [h]	Porte	Door
Verva	Boue	Mire
Vervakère		Miry place
Vère [i]	Oui	Yes
Viage	Voyage	Voyage
Vraic	Algæ	Sea-weed
Verrinnair [k]	Etinceler	To sparkle
Villiannair	Injurier	To injure

[a] *Soulair*, from *soleo*, Latin, to be wont.

[f] *Soudarderie*, a term of reproach, signifying slovenliness, disorder.

[g] *Trepied*, or *terpi*, from *tres pedes*, a three-footed triangle.

[h] *Us*, Old French *huis*, from the Alemannic *us*, whence *uscio*, Italian.

[i] *Vère*, from *vere*, Latin, truly.

[k] From *serre*, glass, to sparkle like broken glass.

The limits of this small work do not allow of a longer selection from the Guernsey Vocabulary as a specimen of the dialect; but the following rhymes, taken from the only book I have ever seen printed in Guernesiais, may amuse and puzzle the curious reader. The work alluded to is, I believe, out of print at present; the title, " Rimes Guernesiais," par un Câtelain.

L'ASSEMBLAIE DÉ PARESSE.

This is a sketch of a parish meeting, convened in the town church, to take into consideration the proposed plan of pulling down Old Fountain-street, and building the present one. It wa formerly so narrow, that in some parts the people could shake hands across the street from the upper stories.

Un matin coum j'etais au marchí[a] dans le skweeze[b],
J'oui la kllìòque[c], qui sounait coum si ch'tait pour l'Eglise;
J'en d'mandit la raison à une femme qui passait,
"Ah! mafai," me dit alle, "ch'est pour pu que j' n'en sait."
Aussitôt j'rencontri un Moussìeu d' Guernezi,
Qui kwarrait[d] coum si l'Gyable[e] ètai souventre[f] li.
"Mais pourqu'est che donc?" jli démande. "Pourqu'estche donc tant d' tripo[g]?
"Nous dirait qu' ch'est l'allarme, et k' l'enmi est ilo[h]."
I' s'arrête un p'tit brin, pour reprendre s'n halaine,
Et mettant ses daeux mains d' chaque côtai d'sa bedaìne[i];
"J'allais scie vous," m'dit-il, "et j'y-allais pour vou keure[k],
"Une assembllìaie d' Pâresse s'en va s'faire toute a l'heure.
"Chest pour affairè d'etat, et n'faut pas y manquair,
"Jusqu'es vìeilles femmes s'en mêlent, et nouz en pâle au fouar[l]."

---

[a] Marchi, *market*.
[b] Skweeze, *crowd*.
[c] Kllìòque, *bell*.
[d] Kwarrait, *running*.
[e] Gyable, *devil*.
[f] Souventre, *after him*.
[g] Tripo, *fuss*.
[h] Ilo, *there*.
[i] Bedaìne, *belly*.
[k] Keure, *to fetch*.
[l] Fouar, *oven*.

R

J'm'en fu donc à l'Eglise vais chu qui s'y passait,
Et j'y vis bièn des gens qu'etaiént là en mouaché^m;
Il y avait la Douzaine et les grands connéta-
    blles;
Des Justiciers ossin, et kìk autres notablles.
I'ságissait d'abattre une route de vieilles maisons,
Pour élargir la rue a l'endrait, où il sont
Des langues de tchifouarait qu'aime a s'ouir ber-
    danguairⁿ
Disaient un tas d'niollin^o coum autant d'ânes-
    begars;
Mais ìl y avait kìkzuns^p quì pâlait assai bien,
Et l'avìs qu'i donnaient est d'accord auve le mien.
Pour ki donc démolir tant d'maìsons en enkair
Où les pères de nos grandpères magaient leur
    soupe de lard?
Où toutes les vieilles bouannes gens, d'leux f'nêtre
    de galtas^r
De chaque côtai d'la rue, sans le moìndre embarras,
S'entre donnaient la maìn —— mais che'nést pas
    d'même acht-heure,
Chu temps là est passai, et le cœur sensiblle en
 . pllièure^s,
Ah paure Rue d'la Fontaine! j'en sie toute en
    colère.
Adì tous tes rakouâins^t! Adi ta varvokère^u!

---

^m Mouaché, *numbers.*   ^r Galtas, *garret.*
ⁿ Berdanguair, *to chatter.* ^s Pllièure, *weeps.*
^o Niollin, **nonsense.**   ^t Rakouains, *corners.*
^p Kikzuns, *some people.*   ^u Varvokère, *mire.*
^q Enkair. *entirely.*

Adì tes bièaux parfums, qui regâlerit les passans!
J'n' les oubllierai jamais, quand je vivrai mes
  chent ans!
Et j'abuserai les gens qui t'éront démolie
En souhaitant leux goule bìen stouffai[x] de bou-
  allie[y].

---

[x] Stouffai, *stuffed.*   [y] Bouallie, *pap.*

THE DOMAILLERIE COTTAGE.

MANY years ago the Domaillerie Cottage was inhabited by an extraordinary old woman unknown to
every one. Whence she came, and who she was, were
enigmas equally insolvable. She was not a native, being
quite ignorant of the language, and only accompanied
by an infant about two years of age; so that her birth-
place, and the cause of her emigration, were secrets
confined to her own breast, and which she seemed in
nowise disposed to trust to any of her neighbours. Her
person was any thing but prepossessing, described as
a tall somewhat stooping figure, with long raven locks
grizzled by time, and large fierce black eyes piercing
from under the shade of a close strange-looking bonnet,
which, together with a brow and face of peculiar expression, completely awed the most venturesome gossip
in endeavours to form the slightest intimacy with the
forbidding stranger.

The cottage now spoken of did not then belong to this
estate, neither was it the same I spoke of in the beginning; but it stood where that tangled mass of ruins
rises from the ivy and briars, that have overgrown
them. It belonged to a person of the name of Dubois,
a foreigner; there was a garden in front, stretching to

the foot of the opposite hill, and hedged high on either
side by a fence of poplars, so thickly entwined with
evergreens as to be impenetrable to every eye, though
overlooked from the summit of the hill now so thickly
wooded.

At the time of Margery's first appearance, some fifty
winters must have passed over her. The child—her
grand child, she called her—was the most beautiful
fairy-like little creature ever beheld, and the old woman
seemed devoted to her charge; it was the only thing
that appeared to interest her, and the love was ardently
returned by the child : never did their nearest neighbour remember to have beheld them apart—no, not for
an instant. How they lived, as no one ever crossed
their threshold, it was impossible to say; but it was
reasoned that, as they could not live without meat, and
meat, however plentiful, was not to be had without
money, they *must* have had something whereon to depend for support, particularly as Margery never sought
employment beyond the house and garden, and that the
child Effie was apparently supplied with every necessary, the best and finest that could be procured. They
were rarely, very rarely, seen beyond the precincts of
the enclosure—still more seldom known to stray further than the wood and valley that surrounded them.
Now, all this was very mysterious, and at first caused
no little stir amongst the gossiping neighbours of St.
Mary's parish; many were the conjectures, the whis-
pers, and ideas set forth upon the occasion; many were
the assemblies round the tea table, or on the "*lit de
fouaille**," at which plans were proposed for the grati-

---

* The green bed—a rural sofa common in every
Guernsey house, composed of the green leaves of the
fern in summer, and dried pea stalks in winter.

fication of their curiosity: all, however, proved abortive, and the taciturnity and chilling aspect of the object of their suspicions being insurmountable, the tumult gradually subsided, and a perplexing shrug, a side-long glance, or bewildered stare, were the only general expressions in which they vented the disappointment of baffled inquisitiveness.

Meanwhile, time swept on in his restless course, and traced many a deeper furrow on Margery's brow, wreathing the raven locks with many a snowy braid, and casting a thicker film across the still bright eye. On Effie it had breathed tenderly—lightly; it had moulded the fairy form to perfect symmetry, given the glowing complexion a more delicate tint, and drawn forth each intellectual power to enlighten and embellish her open countenance. Her large deep blue eyes were mild, and almost sad; and had not a sunny smile ever played round her mouth, they would have given her a decided expression of melancholy. Her hair was of the brightest, fairest hue, falling in rich luxuriant curls on her neck and forehead. Never were two beings more unlike in person and manners than Effie and her grandmother. The bold and haughty demeanour of the old woman melted into humility and sweetness in her child; the stern misanthropy of Margery disappeared in the gentle bearing of young Effie, for, though she never had formed an acquaintance, or joined the sports of the children, who were frequently on the hill and in the wood, yet her pleasant smile, and a few kind words spoken in the sweetest voice, had won all hearts, and she was loved and pitied, as much as her grandmother was feared and detested.

They were often closely watched by the idle school-boys and prying gossips; and it is spoken of as a lovely sight when they were seen together on a summer's evening seated under the fig tree beside their door; old Margery, with one arm placed caressingly round Effie, and the other hand supporting a thick black-looking volume, which she apparently read and explained to her pupil , whose rosy cheek reclined against that dark and pallid countenance, her eyes now gazing earnestly on the wondrous book—now, lifted in their innocence to meet the softened smile of her instructress. It must have been a pleasant sight; and the neighbours often heard too from that lonely dwelling-place the silvery notes of Effie's wild plaintive music, as she sung in the still evenings what seemed to be a foreign hymn.

Sixteen years had passed without any change of place or purpose; the mist that enveloped them was as dark and impenetrable as ever, till it was rumoured that stranger sounds than those of Effie's hymn were heard at night in Margery's cottage. Some one told how they had seen two mantled figures standing at St. Mary's well, and how, upon another evening, Effie was seen alone with the stranger; but by day no trace of him was seen, not the smallest change perceptible for some months. But one night—one calm, soft, autumn night— a piercing shriek ran through the wood: once, only once, the peasant, who was passing, had heard it, yet it thrilled and re-echoed with such fearful sharpness, that it froze his very life blood, and he dared not approach the spot. In the deep silence that succeeded, there was something too appalling to be trespassed on; he returned to his home, and the next morning, on repairing to the spot, old Margery was found seated at the foot of the great white stone beside the well, her hands clasped, her eyes wild and tearless, her cloak half cast off, and her white hair floating loosely on her shoulders. They spoke to her, but she answered not; they lifted her, called her by name, she neither heard nor heeded them; they asked for Effie, and she looked up, shrinking convulsively away, and murmuring " Effie—Effie—love—lost:" then, all at once, she started up, tossed her arms on high, and shouted loudly, " Effie!" then, suddenly darting from them, she rushed to her cottage, whither they did not follow, and nothing more was seen of her until the following morning, when a figure was noticed leaning against the stone, one arm clasped around it, the other concealing the face in the folds of a mantle. The wasted form and streaming hair were not to be mistaken; the neighbours hastened towards the place, accosted, and would have comforted, the old woman, but it was *too late;* that proud heart beat no longer. As the mantle fell from the powerless hand, it disclosed the awful secret. The once flashing eye was fixed and glassy: the lips, compressed into a forced smile, were cold and colourless; death was there, marbling that wasted countenance, and clutching within his remorseless grasp the blighted and broken heart of poor old Margery.

The peasants, shocked and affected at the sight, removed the body: with difficulty they detached the stiffened arm from the stone, and bore her to the cottage; there, on a little table, before an old arm-chair, was the mysterious volume, so often on Margery's knee; it was an English Bible, and on it was a paper, on which the following words were written in a clear bold hand: " Lay me where you find me." This evidently referred to her death, and, accordingly, permission was sought and obtained to fulfil this her last request. She was buried at the foot of the stone, and wept over by many who, during her lifetime, had avoided her with fear; but who now, touched by her misfortune and melancholy end, came voluntarily to pay the last tribute of respect to the remains of the unknown Margery.

The interior of the cottage was found in the neatest order; but nothing that could throw further light on the fortunes or fate of Effie was ever discovered. A heap of paper ashes in the hearth, and the absence of every article of clothing, were all that could increase or explain the mystery that hung over its late inmates. These, as will easily be believed, were repeated, added to, and commented upon, till the most fearful tales were spread concerning it: all that had ever been seen or heard came forth to give its testimony, and to such a pitch did their superstitions rise, that the stoutest hearted peasant would cease his cheerful whistle, hurry his steps, and cast many a timorous glance towards the well, as he crossed the wood on his homeward path. No wonder, therefore, that the Domaillerie so soon fell into decay, and that Dubois gladly parted with it to the owner of the Woodland estate, who built the present cottage, but has never yet persuaded *a native* to inhabit it.

It is said that a tall figure, with white streaming hair and a long cloak, is seen leaning against the stone at certain times, and that voices and unearthly sounds are heard at the well. This has caused the desertion of the sacred fount; for, since that time, no one has presumed to draw its waters, or cull the flowers of that magnolia. St. George's holy well is now the only one in repute; St. Mary's is neglected, and, if not forgotten, remembered but with horror, and avoided with the utmost dread.

LOUISA LANE.

A TALE OF ST. GEORGE'S WELL.

A GUERNSEY LEGEND.

In the early ages, when the Christian saints were in the habit of wandering about the world on knight-errant expeditions for benevolent purposes, armed with all power to bless and to curse, it appears that St. Patrick, from Ireland, and St. George, from England, happened to meet upon this island, and upon this very spot *.

"By the powers," said the Irish saint, crossing himself, "isn't this a purty little island, a jim o' the say, and a mighty agreeable place intirely ! Isn't it a pity its so far off Ireland ? I'm thinking t'would make an illigant place for 'a station;' sure there's plenty of pilgrims would come to it, only for the inconvenience of the wather. But I'll be spaking about it ; at ony rate, I'll just sittle a few monks on it, and make it a snug little farm of my own."

"Not so fast, brother," said St. George, "I've a fancy that way myself: it is really a beautiful spot, and as our rights are equal, you see——"

"Not a bit of it," interrupted St. Patrick, "isn't it an island ?"

"Certainly," said St. George, "what of that ?"

"Why, then, am not I the purticular saint of *all islands*, by the token that I'm King of Ireland? and surely that's an island, God's blessing be upon it, Acushla Machree."

"And so is England," exclaimed St. George, rather impatiently.

"Sorrow a bit of it," says Pat, "sure it's joined to

---

* The estate of St. George, in the Câtel parish, the residence of John Guille, Esq., Bailiff of the Island.

Scotland, and doesn't that make it a *continent ;* you've forgotten your learning brother ——"

" Continent or island," shouted the English knight, who was readier at his sword than at his books, " you've no right to the place, and ——"

I am afraid the saints might have fallen out very seriously upon the occasion, had not the good-tempered knight of the Shamrock, inspired by the wisdom of Solomon, suggested that it should be neither " mine nor thine," but that each should give it its blessing, and go their way, for it would be a burning shame to destroy the peace of the quiet little place, to say nothing of the *sin ;* so St. Patrick struck his staff into the ground, and, signing it with the cross, he declared—" That whilst trees stood and herbs grew, no poisonous thing should ever live upon the face of this earth." And it is remarkable, that from time out of mind, which I suppose is the period alluded to, no venomous insect, viper, snake, or bloated toad has ever been found upon this sacred island.

Then St. George smote a little stream that gurgled by, and behold it sprang up into a deep pure fountain, " the waters of which, he said, should be for the healing of many diseases, and a blessing to the owner of this spot, whose bread should never fail, nor his house be childless, whilst this well was preserved untainted."

Now, many, many years after this, the lord of this estate, an ancestor of the present family, had an only son, about six years of age, to whom the inheritance was to descend, whose life was therefore very precious, and the boy ANDROS was a beautiful and fearless child, with large blue eyes, and fair hair curling after the manner of those days in stiff curls upon his shoulders, as gentle as he was bold, and full of kindly affections; his mother's heart was bound up in him.

Once when a friend of his father's returned from a long sea voyage to the Western Islands, he brought with him a canary bird, which, being very rare at that period, was a most acceptable present to the young lord. The bird became a great pet and plaything; it knew its young master, and fluttered against the bars of its cage in seeming impatience whenever he approached or passed by; but one day whilst the boy was feeding him as usual, the cage door being open, away flew the canary bird through the hall door and into the shrubbery, and away ran little ANDROS after it in the greatest dismay and anxiety.

The bird flew from tree to tree for a long time, so pleased with its liberty that it heeded not the lures of its young master, and at last it flew towards the Holy Well, as the child thought, into the water. He ran to it eagerly, looked down, and saw in the still dark waters beneath, the form of his little favourite, which he hastily bent forward to catch hold of. In this act he must inevitably have fallen in and been drowned, when he was startled and arrested by the neighing of a horse behind him; he looked round, and the fiery head of St George's charger was seen for a moment in the shadow of the deep wood.

That moment saved the boy, for when he turned again for his bird, it was perched upon the cross above the well, singing with all its might, and presently flew back to little ANDROS, and settled upon his hand. St. George is therefore supposed to have interfered for the safety of his protégé, and a picture of the boy and his canary bird may be seen in the hall at St. George amongst the ancestral portraits of the family. Here also may still be traced the ruins of St. George's Chapel, formerly belonging to the abbey of St. Michael, and this ivied well, surmounted by a cross, called the Holy well of St.

George, whose waters are a never-failing remedy for swellings and various affections, known as " Le Mal de Fontaine." Many of the country people now believe in its efficacy, and draw the water in secret, depositing a small piece of money in the niche at the foot of the cross, as an offering to the patron saint.

Superstition also invests it with many terrors, and haunts the beautiful shrubbery with a number of fancied apparitions; even to this day the peasant child goes fearfully along the road after nightfall, where the fire-breathing charger of the famous St. George is seen at certain times careering round the spot which his master has consecrated.

LOUISA LANE.

JERSEY.

—◆—

CHAPTER I.

PASSAGE FROM GUERNSEY TO JERSEY.

ST. OWEN'S BAY—CORBIERE ROCKS—NOIRMONT POINT —APPROACH TO ST. HELIER'S—JERSEY HISTORY— FORT REGENT.

STEAMERS pass almost every day in Summer between the islands of Guernsey and Jersey, and make the passage of sixteen miles and a half in about three hours, and often less. You will leave Guernsey by the steamer, which arrives from Southampton early in the morning, and, if the weather is clear and calm, it will be no small pleasure to survey many of your old haunts as you pass along the eastern coast of Guernsey. The beautiful walks behind Fort George, just visible on the hill side; then the quiet little Fermain Bay; and presently you will see a fleet of small fishing craft lying off Bec du Nez, just under the Monument; whilst as you glance behind there is Castle Cornet, Serk, Herm, and Jedthou, already blending confusedly in the distance.

By this time the Southern precipitous coast opens upon you, but as its details are scarcely discernible, you may for awhile feel that indescribable emotion which every *thinking* mind is apt to be sensible of, on losing sight of a spot

where it has spent pleasant hours, perhaps left a
few kindly hearts. Madame de Staël found travelling " un des plus triste plaisirs de la vie."
Possibly it may be so in one point of view, but like
many other things it depends much upon the object and character of the traveller.

To the mere idler, it is an idleness which ends as
usual in ennui. To the selfish and sentimentalist,
it may frequently be a very kaleidescope of petty
miseries; whilst others pass on in a very *sublime*
indifference, which is not at all enviable. But to
those who take a real *healthful* pleasure in travelling, nothing can be more delightful and profitable; and such an hour as this is one of thoughtful
" gathering into the storehouse of mind that harvest of facts and fancies" which the last field of
research has yielded. Every new place we visit
is, as it were, turning a leaf of the Great Creator's
book.

" Nature is the chart of God, mapping out his attributes:
" Art is the shadow of His wisdom, and copieth His resources."
                    Tupper's Proverbial Philosophy.

And he has not tasted the deepest and best delight of travelling who has not thus turned it to
account.

But you may look ahead now, for Jersey is
doubtless drawing near, and will soon be interesting; it does not give a favourable impression at
its approach from the North and West. That long
line of yellow sand which first attracts attention,
is the Bay of St. Owen's. Towards the close of the
fifteenth century, part, if not the whole, of this
extensive bay was a fertile valley, partially covered

with a forest of stately oaks; but as it was not defended, like the Northern Coast, by a barrier of rocks, it is probable a sudden eruption of the sea inundated the valley, which successive storms laid bare, until little by little the tremendous surf washed away every vestige of the wood. The former existence of this forest is proved as at Vazon Bay, Guernsey, by the frequent discovery of remains of trees at the lowest tide, and by the bed of peat which lies under the sand in this bay. The trunk of one of these trees was found fifteen feet in the main stem, and measured from nine to ten feet in girth; it then branched off, and each of its two limbs were nearly of the same length as the stem itself.

How far this wood may have extended, and whether the cluster of Islands were at one time joined together and formed a peninsula jutting out from the French coast, is a matter of conjecture. There is a tradition that Jersey was *once* so contiguous to Normandy that a feudal lord of the manor in Granville parish held his estate by the tenure of providing a plank for the Bishop of Coûtances to pass over when he visited the Islands *; and another tradition asserts that there was a plank or bridge between France and Jersey, which paid a toll to the Abbey of Coûtances.

---

* This tradition is found curiously corroborated by a similar one in a history of St. Malo; but may not the plank have been for the bishop to pass over, in stepping from *his boat* to the shore, as is the custom at the present day all along that part of the French coast?

s 2

Some little time will now elapse before you reach the next point worth noticing, during which a slight sketch of Jersey History may be interesting.

The History of Jersey.

The island of Jersey is from 12 to 13 miles in length, and scarcely seven in breadth; distant from Guernsey about 21 miles and a half S. S. E.

From Southampton . . .	120 miles.
Weymouth	85 —
Granville	24 —
St. Malo	29 —

Very little can be said of this island previous to the time of Rollo, the first Duke of Normandy, to whom it was surrendered by Charles the Fourth of France, with the Sister Islands, and Normandy itself, in 912.

It appears from the itinerary of the Emperor Antoninus, that the island was known to the Romans by the name of Cæsarea; it is also called Angia, in many old writings, but the name Jersey is a corruption of Cæsarea. For *Ey*, in the language of the northern nations, signified an island; as in the name of *Angles-ey* or Isle of the Angles. And *Jer* or *Ger*, and likewise *Cher*, is but a contraction of Cæsar; as the name of Cherbourg, an ancient sea-port of Normandy, is so called from the Latin *Cæsaris-burgum*. Jersey, likewise, is a corruption of Cæsar's Island.

There are several Roman remains in Jersey, which prove that Cæsar's troops, if not Cæsar himself, were once here. At Mount-Orgueil Castle, there is an old fortification, called to this day *Le Fort de César*. Likewise, at Rozel, in the north of the island, there is a remarkable entrenchment, bearing the traditional name of *La petite Césarée*. Near the manor of Dilament, the remains of a Roman camp may be traced out. Besides the number of Roman coins, which from time to time have been dug up, is evidence enough of Roman conquest.

Previous to the Roman dominion we have the *Cromlechs*, or, as they are called in Jersey, *Poquelayes*, to prove our Celtic origin in both islands. The Druids were famous priests among the Celts and Britons; and the many remains we find of their altars, involve us in their cruel superstition.

However, the limits of this sketch will not permit me to dwell longer on this part of Jersey history : the traveller, if desirous of more information, will find it in Falle's History of Jersey," —a very excellent work, easily procured at the booksellers, or at the Public Library, founded by the author, the Rev. Philip Falle, M. A., a native of the island.

I will briefly notice the position of these islands after the death of Rollo. From this chieftain, six dukes, in succession, retained the sovereignty of the Norman Isles : and then they were attached by William the Conqueror to the British Crown; so that, with the exception of a short period, whilst they were under the government of Robert, his eldest son, their history is of course blended with that of England. . . ..

s 3

France has several times endeavoured to re-possess herself of these little strongholds. Philip Augustus made a sudden and desperate attack upon Jersey; but was repulsed with so much spirit, that King John, who arrived with timely succour, expressed his satisfaction by giving the people of Jersey and Guernsey that constitution which they still value so highly as the Magna Charta of their liberties.

In the reign of Edward the First, the French again invaded Jersey, and were vigorously re-pulsed; which fate they met in two subsequent attempts to conquer it. But, in the reign of Henry the Sixth, Surdeval, a Norman gentleman, with a French force, did contrive to obtain possession of Mount-Orgueil Castle, which they retained for some years, though they never subdued more than half the island.

Philip de Carteret, having secured the Castle of Grasneg, with the aid of a fleet, sent by Edward the Fourth, he retook the fortress, and the French were driven back to the Continent.

The Norman Isles were long faithful to the house of Stuart. During the Commonwealth they resisted the Parliament to the very last, and were the first to proclaim the son of the murdered Charles as rightful Sovereign of England.

Twice did Jersey afford a refuge to its exiled monarch. Charles the Second held his court here during several months; and when he afterwards ascended the throne of his father, he was not un-mindful of his loyal subjects in Jersey. The islanders obtained several privileges, and were presented with a silver mace, with a Latin inscription, acknowledging their loyalty and the services of their leaders, Sir George and Philip de Carteret.

The last attempt of France upon the islands was in 1781, when the French actually landed in the night, and made their way to St. Helier's, without being observed by any one. They surprised the Lieutenant-governor, Major Corbet, in his bed, made him prisoner, and compelled him to sign a capitulation. Two gallant officers, however, disputed the terms; Captain Mulcaster indignantly seized on Elizabeth Castle, determined to defend it to the last; whilst Major Pierson hastily collected all the forces he could and advanced on St. Helier's. In vain did the French general urge the madness of resistance, and entreat him to save the effusion of blood; " Go," said the brave Englishman, " go to your general, and tell him that if he had twice ten thousand soldiers, the troops you have seen are determined, in less than an hour, to drive him from his post."

The island militia did not disappoint the hopes of their leader; they moved on resolutely, and attacked the enemy so impetuously, that the threat was made good, and the French were beaten back, even to their ships, with very considerable loss. Their general, Baron Rullecount, was taken prisoner, and few survivors regained their native shore. The gallant Major Pierson was killed at the commencement of the engagement, and is buried in St. Helier's church, where the States of the Island have erected a handsome

monument to his memory.   Since then we have
enjoyed peace.

And now from the heavy rolling sea, which at
all times is troubled hereabouts, you may know
that you are approaching the

Corbière Rocks.

This fantastic group of rocks forms the south-
west extremity of the island, and is a very dangerous point if the weather be at all rough. This
part of the coast is remarkably precipitous, and a
barrier of enormous sunken rocks extends to a
great distance from the shore; some of them
lifting up their heads as if to warn the mariner
of approach on this side; and others, scarcely
emerging from the great deep, resemble a shoal of
porpoises at play, as the conflicting currents rush
and foam round them even in the calmest sea.
These sunken rocks are more remarkable still on
the southern and eastern coast, particularly off
St. Clement's and Granville.   Soon after passing
the Corbière, you see the lovely Bay of St. Brelade *, the little church, which is the most ancient
parish church in the island, is quite at the water's
edge : whilst a picturesque back-ground is formed
by rock and wood, and by a deep cleft, that runs
up from the shore.

Just above St. Brelade's church stands La Moye
House, formerly the property of the Pipon family ;

---

* St. Brelade, distant five miles from the Royal
Square in St. Helier's.

and next to St. Brelade's, is the little Bay of
Portelet,

Noirmont Point and Tower;

after which the beautiful panorama of St. Aubin's
Bay bursts upon you. At first, the eye only
wanders in delighted surprise over the scene:—it
is so different from the stern barren aspect of the
north and western side of the island. A noble
bay stretches in a fine curve for many miles, with
sloping shores and luxuriant cultivation, studded
with villas, and diversified with woodland. On
the left is St. Aubin's; on the right, St. Helier's,
crouching at the fort of a precipitous hill, which
is crowned by

Fort Regent.

You will have time, before the steamer runs close
behind Elizabeth Castle (which, like Castle Cornet, in Guernsey, is an island fortification, immediately in front of the principal town) to read
a short description of Fort Regent. Mont de la
Ville, or the town hill, rises more than one hundred and fifty feet above high-water mark; and
this fort, which was built in 1806, and is very
extensive, cost the British nation not less than
800,000l. sterling.

It is built of granite, is bomb proof, and covers
more than four acres of ground, having accommodation for five thousand men. All that human
art could do appears to have been called into service to render this fortification inaccessible, with
bastions, half bastions, outworks, and glacis; and
except on the side which faces the sea, with a
ditch, a counterscarp, and covert way, which

encircles it. The well from which the garrison
is supplied with water, is two hundred and thirty
feet deep, one hundred and ninety-five feet of
which is bored through solid rock ; a dozen men
can raise the water into cisterns by means of a
forcing pump, and they can thus bring up about
six thousand gallons per day. You must by all
means walk up to the fort from St. Helier's ; the
prospects are beautiful from different points of
the winding road, and looking from thence downward at the south-east corner of the island, you
will see the vast labyrinth of rocks called *le banc
de violet*, a fearful pass for the mariner.

In levelling the surface of the Town Hill in
1785, a Druidical Temple was discovered, which
the States presented to Marshal Conway, who removed it to his seat at Park Place in Berkshire.

And now, if the tide is up you will pass Elizabeth Castle, (which deserves an especial notice, and
a visit from every stranger); and as soon as you
have entered the spacious harbour, which is a
fashionable and delightful promenade, you may
land without any custom-house annoyances, Jersey being a free port, subject only to a few regulations, and proceed at once to the hotel or board-
ing house you have chosen.

I may here make a few observations on the
climate, language, and coinage of the island, as
these are generally interesting to every visitor.
Jersey, which lies in 49° 16' north latitude, and
2° 22' west longtitude, as nearly as possible midway between Paris and London, is warmer than
any part of England. The mean annual temperature is 52° 20'; the thermometer seldom falling

below freezing point, or rising above 83° in summer; and this absence of cold, rather than any increase of heat, is what gives both these islands so great an advantage over England for invalids and for *flowers.* A flake of snow rarely rests upon the ground after mid-day, and from April to October fires are seldom needed. In the garden, peas may be seen a foot above ground in the end of January, at the same time you may gather narcissus, jonquils, double wallflower, rosemary in flower, myrtle in flower, polyanthus, hyacinth, the primrose and the snowdrop,—all these in gardens where no particular care is taken in the cultivation of flowers, but which is simply sheltered from the most prevalent westerly winds. More rain falls in Jersey than in most parts of England, but less it is believed than in Devonshire and Cornwall. The climate here more resembles that of Penzance; and many medical men have recommended it for consumptive patients in preference to the south of France. I cannot do better here than insert a few extracts from a valuable work by Dr. Hooper on the climate of Jersey: he makes the following observations:—

General Observations.

" The island enjoys an early spring, and a lengthened autumn, vegetation being usually active and forward in March, and the landscape far from naked so late as the end of December. The dreary aspect of winter, then, is comparatively short-lived. But the season of spring is marked by the same unsteadiness of temperature, and harsh variable weather, as in most spots under a similar latitude ; and this disadvantage is particularly felt in May, which often fails to bring with it the expected enjoyments. Generally speaking, our March is mild compared with what it is in neighbouring places, giving a mean temperature nearly three degrees above that of Gosport, and also superior, by about one degree, to Newport, Sidmouth, and Helston. October possesses a still greater superiority in the same respect; consequently, the genial qualities of this climate may be made available to the invalid, to whose case they are applicable, during a period of six months. In diseases, which require the avoidance of great ranges and variations of temperature, the objectionable qualities of the months of April and May, though in a certain degree tempered by the causes which mitigate the severity of our winter, are, nevertheless, such as to call for great care in the use of exercise in the open air. To those who quit warm clothing, or in any other way relax in their precautions against the effects of cold by anticipation, these months too often prove very dangerous. Bating this circumstance, a securer spot could scarce be found by a numerous class of English invalids, within a much greater distance from their homes. The summer is generally, and always comparatively, dry and cool, restricting of course the meaning of the words to the quantity of rain, and the mitigating influence of the surrounding ocean upon the power of the sun's rays. The winter, however, is the season which of all others contributes the most to the peculiarities of this climate. With rare exceptions, it passes off in soft, rainy, or windy weather, with intervals of astonishingly mild days, and with scarcely any frost or snow. Even in the most rigorous years, the latter meteors are far more transitory than in the southern districts of England; and it is indeed quite a memorable event to see snow a foot deep; still more to see it remain on the ground upwards of a week. Although a Jersey winter may appear depressing, and wearisome to some persons, from the absence of

those sports, by which, in colder countries, the rigour
of the season becomes a source of pleasurable excitement
to the healthy; still it must be acknowledged, that, as
respects disease, it cannot but offer many advantages.
By reason of the mildness, trifling range, and variations
of temperature, chronic disorders proceed slowly towards their terminations—a circumstance of no mean
import, since, by allowing more time for the operations
of nature and art, it adds to the chances of recovery, in
cases not absolutely hopeless. As a familiar illustration
of the nature of this climate, I will lay before the reader
some interesting facts, touching the acclimatization of
tropical plants,—from which facts it will be seen, that,
seconded by art, the mildness and equability of atmospheric temperature in Jersey might be, as in fact
it has already been, advantageously applied to the ex-
tension of the vegetable tribes which resist the inclemen-
cies of the northern parts of the temperate latitudes.
Not a few of the more rare shrubs, plants and seeds,
which require stove heat in England, may be grown
here, first in greenhouses, and afterwards transferred to
the open ground. My accomplished friend, Colonel Le
Couteur, of whose shrewdness, and enlightened spirit of
observation, the British public has had sufficient proof,
by his work on the varieties, properties, and classifica-
tion of wheat, lately published, has informed me of his
having succeeded, many years back, in raising a Mesphi-
lus Japonica from seed, which has, ever since, stood out
in the open ground, with the single protection of a bundle of straw, during part of the winter. He has likewise an Acacia, which was brought here from Ceylon.
The Canna Indica ripens its seed constantly under this sky,
as do equally the Ixiæ, many Antholizæ, and Amaryl-
lidæ. Mr. Bernard Saunders's answer to the query I
addressed to him on the same subject, is still more in-

T

teresting. A long and extensive experience has convinced this talented gardener of the propitious qualities of this climate for the naturalization of delicate exotics; and he mentioned several natives of the East Indies, Cape of Good Hope, Brazils, Mexico, New Holland, New Zealand, and China; which, under his own care, have here flowered, and perfected their seeds in the open air, without even the assistance of a wall, or other protection. He doubts not, that many others, if fairly treated, might be added to his list.

The following are those which, from their superior delicacy, have furnished the most striking results:— Lablab Purpureus, Erythrina Cristigalli, Melianthus Major, Vestia Lycioides, Edwardsia Mycrophylla, Cabæa Scandens. The higher and more airy situations on the south-side of the island are undoubtedly those where such experiments are conducted with the best chance of success. In the lower situations, and particularly near St. Helier's, the air is less favourable, being damper, and impregnated with extraneous substances, such as smoke, detrimental to the health of London plants; besides which, a greater exposure to sea-fogs, and greater humidity of soil, by rendering plants more lymphatic, render them more liable to suffer from frost. The months most inimical to exotics in this region are February, March, and April, on account of white frost, and north-east wind; and October and November, by reason of the prevalence of strong westerly gales. From the foregoing facts, it may be concluded, that Jersey presents extraordinary advantages as a medium climate, for the acclimatization of tropical plants, preparatory to similar trials in more northern, and less favoured countries. I have had several opportunities of noticing a fact, which is strikingly in accordance with the latter inference. Persons, who, from a long residence in tropical climates, the East Indies for example, have been rendered incapable of resisting the cold of their native land,—generally experience decided benefit from one or two winters spent in this island. Several cases have come under my observation, of individuals of either sex, from England and Scotland, who, with natural and unreflecting predilection, had, on their return from India, hastened to their native places, but from which, soon after, they were obliged to fly as from almost certain death; and who, having resorted to this milder climate, as a preparatory step, had afterwards returned home, with perfect impunity to health."

Camden says " there is no business in Jersey for the Physicians." I don't know how that can be said in the present day, for there is a formidable list of them to insert, and they all seem to be busy enough ; but probably Falle accounts for this in some degree,—*he* says, that in his time " *intemperance* has produced gout and many diseases ;" intemperance, for which the cheapness of all luxuries affords but too much indulgence, and against which no climate can avail in preserving health. This leads me to notice the current prices of the market, which are still lower than in Guernsey, though not so far differing as to require a separate scale ; you can refer to Chapter X. in the first part of this Guide*.

---

* As to the coinage, both English and French money are in circulation ; the states of Jersey have issued three shilling and eighteen-penny tokens ; and there are bits of copper called liards, of which eight go to the penny, like the Guernsey " Double;" but English money is most

The Language

is French—that is to say, the language of the
court proceedings in the legislature and public
worship is French; but amongst the peasantry,
and even in the private and social intercourse of
the upper class, you will hear a *patois* in which
they delight,—something like the Guernsey
French, and yet so different as to be remarkable
even to the unpractised English ear. However,
of late years the English language has become
more general; it is even taught in some of the
parish national schools, and possibly will soon
supersede French altogether.

CHAPTER II.

ST. HELIER'S—ST. AUBIN'S—ELIZABETH CASTLE—
ST. BRELADE—ST. SAVIOUR'S—PRINCE'S TOWER.

THE first thing a stranger usually does is to make
himself acquainted with the town he is in. St.
Helier's is a pleasant prosperous looking town,
with airy streets, good shops, excellent markets,
but nothing else very remarkable. It was named
after St. Helier, the patron saint of the island,

---

esteemed, and bears a premium, as may be seen in money-
table, Chapter X.

At market, if you purchase an article at the price of
6*d*., you receive a halfpenny back for an *English* sixpence.

who is said to have been murdered by the Normans in one of their piratical excursions. You had better go first to the Royal Square, the centre of business, news, and *gossip;* which has the Royal Court-house on one side, built in 1647, but much altered since then : and the Royal Saloon, Library, and Reading-room will be seen on the right, as you stand opposite the Court-house, by the side of the statue of George the Second, in a Roman military costume. The roads are measured from this spot. This square was formerly the market place, where Major Pierson was killed in gallantly defending the island in 1781.

Close to the Square is the Town Church,

Consecrated in 1341. It is of Norman architecture, and has several handsome monuments. This church is the only one worth examination in the town ; and I shall merely give a list of the churches and chapels hereafter, for those who desire to choose their place of worship.

The Public Baths

Are situated in Bath Street, near the General Post Office. Hot and cold, salt and fresh water, as also shower baths, from seven in the morning till ten o'clock at night. The charges are extremely moderate.

The Hospital

Is situated in Gloucester Street, and was erected in 1783. The apartments are large and airy, with accommodation for upwards of 150 persons. This establishment is supported by a fund raised

from legacies, by a rate levied on all parishes, and
by contributions.

The Prison

Is a handsome building, in an airy spot at the
west end of the town.

The Markets, Halkett Place,

Are excellently well supplied with every kind of
provision, and very cheap. Fish abounds here as
well as in Guernsey, though the market-place
does not show it off to such advantage. Off the
rocks, at Jersey, immense numbers of the conger
eel are caught, some of them *six feet* in length ;
they are in great demand by the lower class, who
salt them for winter use. The fish most in esteem
are the red mullet, of which you may get plenty ;
also abundance of the finest shell-fish.

As soon as possible I would advise you to take
advantage of an ebb-tide, and either walk or ride
to

Elizabeth Castle.

Before visiting this ancient and picturesque fortress the stranger has no idea of its extent ; the
rock on which it stands is no less than a mile in
circumference. The road to it is along a cause-
way across the sand, a little to the right of the
harbour.

Elizabeth Castle was first thought of in 1551,
and a few years afterwards (so says tradition) its
importance became so paramount, that the very
churches were despoiled of their bells, to be converted into funds for the completion of the for-

tress. The ship containing the sacrilegious plunder was lost on its way to St. Malo, which delayed the work until Elizabeth's reign, when it was finished, and received her name. The exiled young monarch, Charles the Second, took refuge here, accompanied by Sir Edward Hyde, afterwards the great Lord Clarendon ; who, it is certain, resided for two years in Elizabeth Castle, and there wrote a part of his celebrated history.

Also, on the summit of a rock, situated a little to the south of Elizabeth Castle, and, like it, accessible at low water, may be seen the rude remains of a hermitage, which was once inhabited by St. Helier. This is, altogether, well worth a quiet visit, for, besides the fortress itself, the splendid view of the bay will delight you.

Another pleasant walk will be to

Fort Regent.

Winding up the road towards the sea, and passing at the back of the Fort, come down upon the west end of the town. I have already described Fort Regent, therefore will proceed, without delay, on some of the country excursions.

The first of these will doubtless be to the pretty little quiet town of

St. Aubin's.

You may sail across the bay at high water, or else walk across the fine sands at low water. Should you prefer the road, which is a very good one, you pass under a hill called Gallows Hill, on which four stone pillars formerly stood, and which served as a place of execution. From St. Helier's to St. Aubin's the scenery is truly beautiful; and the little town itself, which was once the chief place of trade, is strikingly picturesque; it partly skirts the shore, partly lies upon the rocky well-wooded heights, surrounded on three sides by a very fertile country.

It has a small pier, market, and a fortress mounting fourteen guns for its defence. There is no church in St. Aubin; but St. Brelade's Church and St. Peter's, which are both in St. Aubin's parish, are not far distant.

The road to

St Brelade's,

From St. Aubin's, is most charming; ascending the funnel of a narrow valley, after about a mile and a half of varied beauty, you descend into the bay of St. Brelade, and walk to the church, which is the most ancient in the island. It stands on the very edge of the water, which at high tide dashes against the church-yard walls; and a wooded hill rises up behind it, on the summit of which you may again notice La Moye House. St. Brelade's Church, though possessing no architectural ornament, is still a singular and interesting object. In the church-yard stands one of the chapels, which were of an earlier date than any of the churches: it was called La Chapelle des Pêcheurs; and some remains of rude and ancient paintings are observable on the walls. This place, where the first sound of the Gospel was heard— this holy place, where the blessings of Christianity were first learned by the heathen natives, is now a mere *store-house*, for the artillery of the district, a sad specimen of the spirit of the age.

———————

The next walk I shall propose will be in a different direction, and a much shorter one.

St. Saviour's.

To get into St. Saviour's Road you traverse the town towards the north-east, and follow the road up the hill, pausing occasionally to look round and catch a bird's-eye-view of the sea, the town, and Government-house, the residence of the Lieutenant-Governor. About half a mile further on you must enter St. Saviour's church-yard, to look at the extensive and beautiful view of St. Aubin's Bay. The church was consecrated on the 13th of May, 1154, and its cemetery, from its high situation, is a favourite burial-place of the most respectable part of the English residing in St. Helier's and the neighbourhood. In this parish is the free school of St. Manelier, or St. Magloire, founded and endowed by Henry the Seventh; and near it, at a spot called Les Landes Pallot, there formerly stood a rocking stone of great size, so accurately balanced, that it was moved with the slightest touch; it was destroyed some years ago, and broken up for building. Neither holiness nor antiquity seem to be the least respected by our island utilitarians.

Having left the church, proceed onward for

about a mile and a half, and you will find yourself in Gronville parish, at

Hougue Bie, or Prince's Tower,

So called from its having belonged to the Duke
de Bouillon, an admiral in the British navy. This
is the chief elevation of the island; and from the
summit of the tower the eye wanders delightedly
almost over the whole island. Jersey, from hence,
appears like an extensive pleasure-ground—an
immense park, beautifully undulating, and studded with villages and cottages. You cannot but
feel an irresistible desire to explore those valleys
and ravines; to wander about those pastures and
orchards, and descend into the quiet bays and
creeks, unshackled by the noise of a jaunting car,
and the directions of an officious cicerone. No—
no—as in Guernsey so in Jersey, be independent
of all guides and guide-books. After the first few
days, when you get accustomed to the map, and
have paid the matter-of-course visit to each of the
lions, go by yourself, and seek as your fancy leads
you for those innumerable beauties which have
never been described; no where will you find a
richer field for solitary enjoyment than in this
beautiful island.

Prince's Tower,

Where you are now standing, is raised upon an
artificial mound, covered with evergreen and
flowering shrubs. In the months of August and
September there are numbers of magnificent hydrangeas in blossom, the flowers of which are
immense, and mostly of a rich or a pale blue.

The origin of La Hougue Bie is traditionary from the " Livre Noir de Coûtances," which tells us how, in bygone times, *long, long ago,* a monstrous serpent or dragon infested this part of the island, devouring every living being within its range, until the terror-stricken inhabitants knew not how to escape its voracity. Now it happened, that somewhere on the Normandy coast, a noble knight named De Hambie heard of the fame of this monster, and resolved to attempt his destruction. The knight was bold and strong, and taking with him but one hitherto trusty servant, he set forth on his expedition, to conquer or die. The heroic Norman succeeded in destroying the dragon; but he returned not again to the home where his lady anxiously watched for him day and night; he never saw his native land again, or wore the honours of his victory.

The servant he had chosen for his companion had conceived a passion for his noble mistress, and thirsted for the possessions of his master. De Hambie was murdered by him as he slept in extreme weariness, after the contest with the dragon, and the servant returned to Normandy with a well-told tale of his lord's death, and with a solemn declaration that in his dying moments he had expressed a wish that his widow should bestow her hand upon his favourite servant. After some time of great mourning, the Lady De Hambie fulfilled her husband's request ; but the guilty conscience of the murderer gave him no peace, no rest,—he was a miserable man ; and, at last, in a fit of delirious despair, he uttered such

cries of remorse that the truth was suspected.
Little by little they drew from him the whole
confession of his treachery, and he suffered the
death he so well deserved. The widow of De
Hambie, in proof of her fidelity to the memory
of her lord, caused this immense mound of earth
to be erected over the spot where he was murdered; and, on the mound a tower and chapel, of
so great a height that she could see it from her
own Castle at Coûtances.

Many years afterwards, Richard Mabon, having
on his return from Jerusalem been appointed to
the deanery of the island by the Bishop of Coûtances, made many alterations, and added to the
chapel, which he called the Chapel of Notre
Dame, or our Lady of Hougue Bie. He also
took advantage of the credulous islanders by ex-
hibiting miraculous lights in a cavern, which he
excavated in imitation of the Holy Sepulchre at
Jerusalem; wherein he placed a figure of the
Virgin Mary, and encouraged every species of
Romish superstition, till it even became a by-
word to say of any thing very marvellous that it
was a miracle of La Hougue Bie.

CHAPTER III.

THE road from St. Helier to Gorey is scarcely less
beautiful than that from St. Helier to St. Aubin;
with more variety of inland and sea views.
You can hire a car, intended for four or for six
persons, at about seven shillings per day, or you
may walk, for the distance is not above four miles,
to Mont Orgueil Castle. Passing through George
Town, about a quarter of a mile from St. Helier's,
the road does not skirt the sea shore, but passes
through a rich low country, then turning to the
left it ascends a steep hill, and presently drops
down upon the

Church and Hamlet of Grouville.

The church—the parsonage—three or four
houses, and a few cottages scattered round about,
and mingled with gardens and orchards, form one
of the prettiest landscapes in the island.

Gorey.

Very soon after this you see Mont Orgueil
rising in the distance, with the little town of
Gorey sitting at its feet, and though apparently
this is but a mere village, it is of considerable
importance as the seat of the oyster fishery. This

U

fishery is the chief support of Gorey, and supplies the English market at Colchester to a large extent. Upwards of two hundred and fifty boats are employed, with as many as fifteen hundred sailors, besides nearly a thousand persons, chiefly women and boys, in matters connected with the fishery. It is a most animated scene from the 1st of October to the 20th of May, particularly when on a fine spring afternoon the fleet of fishing-boats in full sail bear down towards their rendezvous. Many disputes have arisen and indeed exist between the English and French authorities respecting the fishing boundaries; which are not very clearly defined, as the oyster beds lie near the French coast.

Mont Orgueil.

The greatest attraction in this neighbourhood is Mont Orgeuil Castle, which well deserves its name. Proudly it stands upon a rocky headland, jutting out into the sea, frowning as it were upon the everlasting waters which seem to mock its ruined walls. The old grey towers and buttresses are mantled with luxuriant ivy, and many of the fortifications are yet entire. Climb up their steep ascent by the broken flight of rocky steps, you will be richly repaid for the fatigue by the magnificent prospect. Grouville Bay on the right—St. Catherine's Bay on the left—a richly wooded range of heights—the village beneath, with its tiny harbour and Lilliputian fleet—then, far beyond, the whole expanse of ocean, and, if the day is clear, even the villages and cathedral of Coutance, on the French coast, may be seen with the naked eye.

This castle in ancient days was a very important place. Its origin and builder are unknown, though its foundation is assigned to Robert, the eldest son of William the Conqueror. In the reign of King John its fortifications were strengthened and enlarged, and it subsequently received many additions, which are recognized by the different coats of arms engraved on stone escutcheons and placed over several of the gateways. Charles the Second inhabited this castle for some months after the death of his royal father, and "King Charles's room" is still in tolerable repair, and the frequent resort of picnic parties.

The well-known Prynne was a prisoner here from August, 1637, to November, 1640. While in confinement he celebrated it in verse—"A Poetical Description of Mont Orgueil Castle, in the Isle of Jersey, interlaced with some brief Meditations from its rocky, steep, and lofty situation."

Yet these are not the most interesting facts connected with this ancient place. Tradition tells us that its present name was given by Henry the Fifth's brother, the Duke of Clarence, who, whilst he was encamped in the neighbourhood of Coutance, took notice of this stately tower, and being curious to see it nearer, he made an expedition to the island, and was so much struck by the commanding situation and strong defence of Gorey Castle (as it was called), that he bestowed a more honourable name upon it, and interested his bro-

ther Henry on its behalf, from whom [Mont
Orgueil received several improvements.

Falle, in his Jersey History, gives a long and
interesting account of the taking of this castle by
Surdeval, a Norman gentleman, acting under the
orders of Peter de Brezé, Count de Maulevrier,
who held it in his power, and the island in his
fear, for six years; without, however, obtaining
obedience from more than six parishes.   The
other six were kept in defiance of him, by Philip
de Cartaret, a brave Seigneur de St. Ouên, who
fortified himself in the western Castle of Grosnez,
and with indefatigable zeal, aided by an English
fleet under Sir Richard Harliston, so blockaded
and harassed the garrison.of Mont Orgueil, that
it yielded it last, on the failure of a stratagem
which the besieged had hoped would bring them
succours from France.

The stratagem was this:—When the garrison
of Mont Orgueil was reduced to the greatest
extremity by want of food and ammunition,
it was proposed to attempt the building and
launching of a boat, which should endeavour to
pass through the English fleet on some very dark
night. To deceive their besiegers more effectually,
they built *two* boats, one on the ramparts, pur-
posely but half concealed, the other near it, but
quite out of sight. The workmen so ordering
their blows, and striking so evenly together, that
from the sound no one in the camp could suspect
the building of two boats, they expected to launch
one of them before the enemy was on the alert at
the disappearance of the other.

Very possibly they would have succeeded, as
the islanders were quite content with watching
the progress of the visible boat, but in one of the
many skirmishes and sorties the French had
taken prisoners, one of whom contrived to shoot
an arrow from the castle to the camp having a
letter tied to it, which betrayed their plan.

This information was given the very day the
boat was to be sent forth, consequently it had
hardly rested upon the water, and glided a few
lengths from the shore, when it was intercepted.
All hope of relief being now destroyed, the distressed garrison surrendered, and, amidst the
shouts of a delighted multitude, the royal standard of England once more floated in triumph
over the castle.

I have detained you a long time at Mont Orgueil, without giving its full history, but for this
I must refer you again to Mr. Falle.

Anne Port.

Anne Port is a small cove close to Mont Orgueil, near which is a cromlech or poquelay,
being a rough slab of rock, placed horizontally,
and supported by several smaller pieces. The
large stone measures three feet thick, ten broad,
and fifteen long. This is the largest single block
of Druidical monuments now remaining in the
island. It is equal in dimensions to the celebrated cromlechs at Poitiers, in France.

The insulated tower, called Archirondal Tower,
stands out picturesquely on the southern point of

St. Catherine's Bay,

Near which is an ancient chapel, in a very ruinous condition. There is nothing to detain you from the loveliest bay in the island, that of Rozel, unless you ascend a small cliff, close to the harbour, called

Le Couperon,

And there observe one of the most extensive Druidical antiquities, supposed to have been a temple.

Rozel Bay.

However, there is nothing better worth visiting than this beautiful little inlet or creek. It is hemmed in by high cliffs; deep wooded glens branch from it to the interior; there is a little harbour too, and a few fishermen's cottages scattered round the beach, and some dilapidated barracks not far distant. This is a favourite spot for picnics, and many a flirtation has been brought to a *crisis* under the influence of Rozel's secluded and pleasant walks, whether by the precipitous pathway which overhangs the ocean, or by the tangled foot-tracks along its thickly wooded valley.

Here, if you are weary, you may rest, and procure refreshment in a cleanly comfortable room in the afore-mentioned barracks.

223

CHAPTER IV.

TRINITY—ST. JOHN'S PARISH—BONNE NUIT—MONT
MADO, &c., &c.

TRINITY is one of the northern parishes, and the
new road runs directly to its church from St.
Helier's. When I say the *new road*, I mean those
wide macadamized roads which intersect the island
in all directions, and which Jersey owes to the
public spirit of one of its late governors, Sir
George Don. That they are an immense improvement to the country, and of great advantage
to the people, no one can for a moment doubt ;
yet, you as a stranger, desirous of exploring a
new and beautiful island, will entirely fail of your
purpose if you *confine* yourself to these high roads.
The ancient ways of our forefathers must be
trodden if you would attain to any real knowledge
of the people and the place. These roads, or more
properly speaking, lanes, for they are extremely
narrow, winding, and overhung with trees, ramify
through the length and breadth of the land, in
countless numbers; they branch off in every direction, touch at every church, every farm-house,
every bay, and every point. It is objected, that
they are too circuitous, and that they are so shut
up with high banks and over-arching trees, that
nothing can be seen. As to the first, certainly if
you are in a hurry, I strongly advise you to avoid
all *seemingly* short cuts by shady lanes; they will

take you to the desired spot, I dare say, but they
will also go their own way, and a weary winding
way it will be to a *man in haste*.

As to their high banks, &c., nothing is more
delightful on a hot summer's day than to wander
for hours in these cool pleasant lanes, where the
sweetest flowers stud the banks, and luxuriant
ivy spreads on either side its variegated leaves,
climbing up the old trees, and throwing fantastic
wreaths from branch to branch. Besides, every
now and then, lest you should tire of the quiet
dells, the lane rises up to the summit of some
rugged hill, and such beautiful vistas are laid
open as it is worth a longer walk to see. In these
lanes, also, you may observe more accurately the
habits of the people, they make as much or more
use of their old roads as of the new, and you will
pass through their richly-laden orchards, their
pasture-lands, where the Jersey cow is preparing
for the English market,—the farm-yards, so unlike those of England,—and find more subjects of
interest and beauty than any *guide-book* can describe or direct you to.

You are now on your way to Boulay Bay;
passing by Trinity Church, which was consecrated
September 3rd, 1163; it has nothing remarkable,
neither will you discover much of the remains of
that Roman entrenchment, called

La Pétite Césarée, or Cæsar's Wall,

Which lies in this parish. At a short distance
from the chrch, which is about three miles from
St. Helier's, you will find the *grandest* bay in the

island. The contrast is very striking between the inland scenery and the bold, precipitous, naked coast of

Boulay Bay,

From whence you look out upon the Channel Sea, and have a view of the islands of Guernsey, Alderney, and Sark, as well as of the coast of France. The government has long had an idea of erecting on some part of the Jersey coast a naval station, which in time of war would not only protect the trade of the Channel, but form a convenient point of observation on the movements of the French from Cherbourg to Brest.

Boulay Bay seems to offer the greatest advantages for this object. It has a good anchorage, an easy access and a considerable depth of water, when all other bays of the island are dry. Several surveys have been made, and soundings taken, and very likely at no distant period there may be an extensive pier and breakwater completed, and employed as a naval station.

If you are a botanist, it is worthy of remark, that the heath on this side of the island far excels both in tint and size the blossom of any of the wild heaths of Britain.

The next parish to this is

St. John's Parish.

Its church is five miles from St. Helier's, and was consecrated on the 1st of August, 1204.

A short distance from the church, a path leads down to the little harbour of

Bonne Nuit,

Where there are barracks, neatly constructed, and almost untenanted since the conclusion of the war. The principal thing to see in this parish is Mont Mado. There are several quarries of granite about three quarters of a mile to the north of the church, which deserve to be visited. The cliffs from which this beautiful and durable stone is obtained are very extensive. Mont Mado quarry is held in most esteem, being the whitest, and perhaps of the hardest quality; it also splits asunder with great regularity and beauty; most of the public buildings and gentlemen's seats are faced with it.

In this parish there are two or three good inns, especially one near the church, where you may be refreshed, and rested before you return to St. Helier's, or proceed further.

I think that for a single person, a pedestrian, it would save much time and trouble if he *did not* return every day to St. Helier's, but took a bed at any of these places; they·are very clean and comfortable, and then he is already on the spot for a fair start the next morning to the caves of Grêve de Lecq and Plémont. However, as most people will not take my advice, *I* must go back to the town, and proceed in an orderly manner to the next chapter.   ·

CHAPTER V.

THE road to St. Peter's branches off from St.
Aubin's road on the right, after passing Mill-
brook, and in less than a mile further you will
enter St. Peter's Valley.

This is really a beautiful spot, whether you
ascend or descend; often may you pause to look
back with delight at the quiet scenery of this
deep dell. The thick foliage of the wooded hills
on either side shadowing a green pasturage, through
which a little playful rivulet runs murmuring
sweet music—groups of picturesque cottages, and
cattle feeding on the hill side or in the meadows.
No one would willingly pass hastily through this
pleasant valley, where you might believe yourself a hundred miles from the sea-coast you are so
near.

St. Peter's Church,

Which is four miles from St. Helier's, is one of
the best in the island, consecrated in 1167, on the
29th of June. Its spire, which is the highest in
Jersey, was many years ago injured by lightning,
but has since been repaired. On one of the buttresses at the west end are engraved several black-
smiths' implements, respecting which I can give
no information. Some suppose it was the work

of some pious smith, who thus displayed his ingenuity in what he considered *ornamenting* his church; but more probably it was some ingenious idler perpetuating his *idleness*.

The School of St. Athanasius.

Or, as Falle says, of St. Anatase, is in this parish; it was endowed for the benefit of the children belonging to the six western parishes of the island, and was founded by Vincent Jehy, a native of Jersey, in the reign of Henry the Seventh. The number of scholars is seldom more than half a score; the annual revenue is said to be about twenty-five pounds sterling.

St. Lawrence.

St. Lawrence is the next parish westward of St. Peter's, and has many beautiful walks; but there is nothing to which I can particularly direct you, except the church, consecrated in 1199, on the 4th of January. It has neither steeple nor tower, though it once most likely had both, and internally presents a heterogeneous mixture of painted and circular arches of simple and ornamental reliefs; the eastern windows are light, and were formerly embellished with painted glass; much of this has been broken, and repaired at random.

St. Mary's Parish

is remarkable only for a few chalybeate springs, and some romantic walks, which are very little frequented. The church was consecrated on the 5th of October, 1320, and has been suffered to fall out of repair, greatly to the reproach of the parish. On leaving it, you enter a winding valley, which leads you to St. Ouen's parish, and the beautiful caves of Grevè de Lecq and Plémont. Grevè de Lecq is not a bay, but a cove, approached by a narrow deep valley, and bounded by nearly perpendicular cliffs, which the ceaseless fretting of the sea has undermined into deep caves, one of which, though of no great height, is a hundred feet in length. This subterraneous passage cannot be explored when the tide is up; and, when down, the approach is rendered somewhat difficult by the quantity of pebbles forced by the waves into the mouth of the cave. The best way of visting the caves is by water. With a boat from Grevè de Lecq it would be easy to land at every opening in the cliffs; this would avoid scrambling over masses of rock, or winding along narrow paths that skirt the edge of the precipices; but some persons would *prefer* the scramble, and the dizzy downward track; if so, they may thoroughly indulge their propensity all along this coast, even to the promontory of Plémont.

Plémont is. almost an island, from being so deeply intersected on either side, and joined to the land by a very narrow isthmus. Over the deep fossé is a drawbridge, and close to it is a guardhouse. The rock, on one side of the drawbridge, drops in nearly a perpendicular line to the sea, whilst another rises up two hundred feet above the water absolutely vertical, and glowing with a splendid variety of tints in the summer

x

sunlight. This place is also celebrated for its caves; the declivity on the eastern side, though steep, is safe; you *may* go down the hill which covers them, but it is considered a dangerous path.

The opposite promontory to Plémont is that of Grosnez, where you will find the ruins of a castle famous in Jersey history. A small gateway, and two projecting angles, which constitute the remains of a portal, loose fragments of stone scattered about, denote that the original circumference of the walls must have been extensive; but nothing more is visible of Grosnez Castle; nothing even is known of its architect or foundation. It is certainly very ancient: I find it spoken of in the " Chroniques des Iles, par George S. Syvret," as a strongly fortified castle in the reign of King John, belonging to one Philip de Carteret; and in Henry the Sixth's reign it was still a notable place, as being the stronghold which the brave Seigneur de St. Ouen, Sir Philip de Carteret, held out against the French, when they had possession of Mont Orgueil for six years, as I have related elsewhere. The De Carterets are one of the noblest and oldest families in the island; their first title to the Seigneurie of St. Ouen is beyond record; certainly Phillippe de Carteret, in 1585, was then the fifty-ninth Seigneur of that name, and a very interesting story is connected with this castle and family, which is worth remembering as you stand upon these heights amid the ruins of Grosnez.

The Lady of St. Ouen's.

In the reign of Henry the Seventh one Matthew Baker was appointed Governor, or " Capitaine " of Jersey, a tyrannical malicious man, who practised all manner of extortion on the poor islanders, and was more than once summoned before the court by the Seigneur of St. Ouen, to whom the oppressed people appealed for redress. This caused a mortal hatred between Baker and De Carteret; but because the latter was a noble and upright gentleman, the Governor could find no pretext for an open quarrel; and his dark thoughts at length wove a web of falsehood which he hoped would entangle his enemy effectually.

He wrote a letter in the name of Sir Philip de Carteret to certain noblemen of Normandie, offering to betray the island to the French for certain considerations, which letter he threw into a dry ditch near Longueville, a spot which Baker passed frequently in going from the Castle to St. Helier's, and, causing one of his followers to pick it up, he rode straightway to the royal court, and proclaimed the Seigneur of St. Ouen a traitor to King and country.

The bailiff of the island, Clement Le Hardy, was in league with the Governor, and gave a ready belief to the accusation. The follower, also, who had picked up the letter, by name Rogier Le Boutillier, was a bold bad man, whom Sir Philip had once saved from the gallows, and he loudly supported the charge, offering to give battle to the

accused, as a false traitor. Sir Philip De Carteret
was seized and thrown into a dungeon of Mont
Orgueil Castle; Le Boutillier was also sent there,
to abide until St. Lawrence's day, 1494, which was
the day fixed for this mortal combat, but with
this difference, that whilst Le Boutillier was well
fed, and had freedom to go where he pleased about
the castle, the noble knight was closely impri-
soned, and life scarcely sustained by the coarse
food they gave him. Meantime, the Governor, to
make sure of his enemy, set off to London to lay
his story before the King in council, first of all
issuing an edict jointly with the bailiff, that no
vessel or boat should leave the island without a
special permit, lest any of De Carteret's friends
should get the start of him and frustrate his
plans.

At this period Margaret de Harliston, the young
wife of Philip de Carteret, was at Grosnez Castle,
in childbed with her first child; she heard that
her husband was a prisoner in Mont Orgueil—
he was accused by the tyrant Governor of treason
to his King—he, the loyal, faithful De Carteret,
who had fought at his father's and *her* father's
side for the defence of his country, when none
else dared stand against the French invaders
under De Brezé—he was accused of such foul
treason by his greatest enemy, without one friend
daring enough to help him. She rose up from her
couch, and, as the old Chronicle says, " Se con-
fiant totallement en Dieu, qui est le vraye support des pauvres affligés." She left her little son,

scarcely a week old, and, alone with one of her own boatmen, she crossed the sea on a dark stormy night, resolved to defend her husband's honour before the King himself.

She arrived safely at Guernsey, and learnt that the Governor Baker had just passed on to England; then accompanied by William de Beauvoir, a friend of De Carteret, she set sail immediately after him, and through great peril arrived at Poole, whilst Baker was still in the town, even on the very quay. They would now have surely been discovered had not, by the mercy of God, ("comme Dieu voulut, ayant toujours soins des siens"), a storm of hail and wind driven the Governor and his attendants into shelter, during which the Lady of St. Ouen was safely landed, and hospitably received in secret by a gentleman named De Havilland.

Notwithstanding her great fatigue, this noble lady would not rest, but, as soon as possible, she mounted a horse and rode to Salisbury, from thence, with as little delay as possible, to London, and being kindly protected by the Bishop of Winchester, Dr. Fox, who was a member of the Privy Council, and in great esteem at Court, she obtained an early audience of the King, pleading with all the eloquence of woman's love that her husband should be fairly heard, and calling to mind his many services and loyal family, till Henry not only inquired minutely into her story, but granted her an order for her husband's instant release before he even heard the Governor's accusation.

x 3

Hardly had Margaret left the Royal presence when she met the astonished Governor on the stairs, and he did not recover from his surprise before he was ushered into the council chamber, and overwhelmed with reproaches and disgrace.

As to the Lady of St. Ouen's, hastening back to Jersey with her kind friend De Beauvoir, she arrived the night before St. Lawrence's Day, just in time to save her beloved husband from a certain and treacherous death; for the coward villain Le Boutillier had caused pitfalls to be dug on the ground appointed for the combat, so that his enemy might fall unawares and assure to himself the victory.

Soon after this Matthew Baker was removed from the government of Jersey, and was succeeded by Thomas Audrey, a good and loving friend to Sir Philip De Carteret, and to his eldest son Edward, after him. The Lady of St. Ouen, after living in great happiness with her noble husband about nineteen years, was left a widow with eleven sons, who all rose to honourable places, some in their native island, some at the Court of England. One of them, Jean de Carteret, being page to Sir William Compton, First Lord of the Bedchamber, and one of the Privy Council, was a great favourite of his master, "car il estoit fort léger à courrir et à saillir, il franchissoit 24 ou 25 pieds tout d'un sautt; il étoit merveilleusement disposé de ses membres, tant pour la lutte que pour toute autre chose, qu'il ne trouvait guère son pareil."

Thus prospered the family of this fearless and faithful Lady De Carteret *.

The church of St. Ouen's was consecrated on the 4th September, 1180; is situated in a lonely part of the parish, and seems to have sunk into the earth, as the principal entrance goes down two steps, and the door-case is unusually low. Possibly the sand may have drifted in the violent storms to which this coast is exposed, and caused this appearance.

---

* A new cave has very lately been discovered under the archway of Grosnez, with some interesting antiquities. A quarry being opened for Mr. Le Gros, the labourers accidentally struck upon a hollow sounding rock, which, when further examined, proved to be the entrance to one of the largest caves, and in which the remains of a human skeleton, fragments of armour, and broken swords were found. These curiosities have been carefully removed, and the cave is open to visitors; but some fear is entertained that, by this excavation, the safety of the old archway is endangered.

CHAPTER VI.

THE road to St. Clement's parish from St. Helier's
is chiefly along the south-eastern coast, which
gives you a fine view of those dangerous rocks
called Le Banc de Violet, running round La
Rocque Point, upon which the French under
Rullecourt effected a landing in the year 1781.
Seymour Tower is also a conspicuous object,
situated among these rocks at a distance of two
miles from the land at high water, but may be
approached when the tide is low. It is exposed
to a tremendous sea during the winter storms,
which literally overwhelms it in spray and foam.

Pontac is a place of great resort for picnic
fishing parties, and in the fine summer nights
crowds of people assemble on the shore at low
tide to catch sand eels, which are raked up,
hooked out, and scrambled for in quantities, with
no small amusement. I have never been one of a
lançon party in *Pontac*, but in Sark and Guernsey
often, and it is a most picturesque scene at all
times; but above all, on a clear moonlight evening, as the groups assemble in fishing costume,
silently beginning at the edge of the ebb tide,
when the waves are gently breaking on the shore,

and the silvery fish are wriggling through the furrowed sand ; then growing eager as the waters rise, peals of merry laughter ring round the bay— baskets are filled—the rake and the hoe ply faster, till the upcoming tide drives off the light-hearted heavy-laden plunderers to make a good supper on the delicious lançons, and pick out the best for to-morrow's market.

If you have the opportunity, by all means go to a moonlight fishing, either here or in Sark, where it is more picturesque and delightful from the nature of its beautiful bays, and the excitement of scrambling down an awful precipice by the fitful light of the moon.

Vraicing.

The harvest of sea-weed, called in French *varech*, and in Jersey and Guernsey *vraic*, is a busy time, which continues for about ten days at two seasons of the year, beginning on the 20th of July and the 10th of March. This vraicing is much the same thing as in Guernsey, where I have fully described it; but the vraicing cakes, made of flour, milk, and sugar, are more plentifully partaken of in Jersey, and the merry-making is as busy, as noisy, and as amusing to witness.

The sea-weed is used as fuel and manure ; wood is burnt in very small quantities, and coal scarcely at all used, except on high days and holidays, at flaunchades or betrothals, weddings or christenings, when the best little parlour fire is lighted, and the "gossips," *visines* as they are called, assemble to drink tea and eat *Gâche à Corinthe* (an excellent thing).

The church of St. Clement, consecrated in 1117, is a neat building, in tolerably good repair. About three quarters of a mile from the church is the Manor of Saumarez, formerly belonging to the Dumaresq family, now the Seigneurie of the Hammonds.

This island has many very ancient families, mostly of Norman and Breton origin, and these, possessing the principal Manors or Seigneuries (for they are not all of the same dignity), had the same civility paid them as in France, of not being addressed by their family-name, but by that of their Seigneurie, which gave them a certain distinction. Latterly this has fallen into disuse; but, not many years ago, the different branches of the *De Carteret* family were known as the Seigneurs de St. Ouen, de la Trinité, de Vinchelez, &c. That of *Bandinel*, the Seigneur de Melesche; that of *Dumaresq*, la Dame de Saumarez, Seigneur des Augrés; that of *Lemprière*, Seigneur de Dilament; that of *Pipon*, the Seigneur de Noirmont, &c. The last of the Dumaresqs of Saumarez was Deborah, daughter and heiress of Philip Dumaresq, who presented James the Second with a manuscript account of the Channel Islands, and their best means of approach and defence. This was kept as a state secret till about the close of the last century, when it was transmitted to Admiral D'Auvergne, the then naval commander on this station, which directions have been very highly prized, and may be useful to publish more generally.

Directions for Approaching the Island of Jersey from the Northward or England, by Philip Dumaresq, Seigneur de Saumarez. 1685.

Sailing southward along the Bay of St. Ouen (the westernmost of the island) there is good anchorage in the bay, with an easterly wind, in 12 or 15 fathoms of water for great ships, and in 7 or 8 for lesser, but no harbour for great or small, only a creek for fisher boats, called L'Etac.

If you come to an anchor in this bay, leave about two-thirds thereof to the northward of you.

The north and south parts of the bay are full of rocks, but the middle is clean. *La Frouquie* is a rock that seldom covers, and all the ground betwixt it and the land is rocky.

In sailing about the *Corbière* to come into *St. Aubin's Bay*, keep off from the land about half a league, and sail westerly till you see the point called *Portelet*. Then you may run close along the shore without danger, till you come near *Noirmont Point*, which you must keep with the *Corbière*, leaving it open, till you see two single houses among some trees upon the east side of *Noirmont Hill*, in a valley between the point and *St. Aubin*. Then bear into the roads, fearing nothing, and come to anchor in two, three, or four fathoms at low water.

At half-flood you may run with a ship of two or three hundred tons over all the rocks except *Silly Rock* and *Hinguette*, which do not cover till about two hours flood.

There is also a good channel between *La Rodandière* and *Hinguette*. If you go through, keep the *Gallows* and the west walls of *Elizabeth Castle* one by the other, or in a line, till you see a *White House* standing alone over the top of the *Tower of St. Aubin*. Then run in, and anchor in two, three, or four fathoms water at low tide.

As for the tides, it is high water here at six o'clock upon the change and the full of the moon.

From *Grosnez Point* to the *Corbière* the current sets south from half-ebb to half-flood, from which time to half-ebb again it sets north.

From the *Corbière* to *La Rocque* the current sets east all the time of the flood, and west during the ebb. It is the same along the north coast of the island.

In this parish of St. Clement there is a small estate, which was bestowed by Charles the Second on the present proprietor, who was fishing on the coast, and had with him a grey horse, on which he had the honour of landing that prince from the boat the first time he visited the island. By the tenure of this estate, the owner is bound, whenever the King comes to the island, to provide a horse of the like colour for the same occasion.

A Table of Distances, from the Royal Square to different Places in the Island, will be found very useful to Pedestrians in their wanderings over it:—

	Miles.	Furlongs.	Yards.
To St. Clement's Church........	2	4	66
Grouville Church............	2	6	66
Gorey	4	1	0
Mount Orgueil	4	6	33
St. Saviour's Church	1	2	99
St. Martin's Church	3	6	66
Rozel Barracks	5	6	0
Trinity Church	3	6	0
Boulay Bay	4	6	0
St. Peter's Church	4	6	4
St. Ouen's Church	6	2	0
St. Lawrence's Church	3	2	0
St. John's Church	5	5	68
St. Mary's Church	5	6	0
St. Brelade's Church	5	4	0
St. Aubin's Pier	3	6	132

CHAPTER VII.

LEGISLATURE—QUEEN'S OFFICERS—MILITIA—PLACES OF PUBLIC WORSHIP—PUBLIC INSTITUTIONS—SCHOOLS—NEWSPAPERS—BOATMEN'S FARES—AND MONEY TABLE.

THE legislative power in Jersey resides in an assembly called the STATES; the Royal Court, as it is called, consists of a president, termed the Bailli of Jersey, who is appointed by the King, and

Y

twelve judges, who are elected for life by the people. All heads of families paying parochial rates being entitled to vote, these judges or jurats are elected by almost universal suffrage, and causes a degree of party spirit, which is greatly to be lamented. It is impossible to conceive the extent to which this evil is carried, and from which the sister island Guernsey is almost wholly free. Jersey is divided into two factions, calling themselves the Laurel and the Rose, which hold themselves as distinct one from the other as if they were of different countries or hostile nations; the spirit pervades not only public business, but affects even private society and tradesmen in their customers. The States, as a legislative body, have also the rectors of the twelve parishes, the twelve constables of the twelve parishes elected by the people every three years, the King's officers—le Procureur du Roi and the King's Advocate, who are appointed by the King, with other officers, and six Advocates, in the nomination of the Bailli.

The present governor of the island is—

The Right Hon. William Carr Beresford, Baron of Albuera and Dungarvon, in the county of Waterford, G.C.B., G.C.H., &c., &c.

Lieut.-Governor and Commander-in-Chief of the Forces in the Island— His Excellency Major-General Sir Edward Gibbs, T.E., C.B.

Governor's Office, Anne Street, open from ten o'clock in the morning till four in the afternoon. Passports are granted (gratis) at this office to persons going to France, as also at the French Consul Office, 3, Halkett-place.

Bailli of Jersey—Sir John De Veulle, Knt.
Dean—The Very Reverend Dr. Jeune, D.C.L.,
Rector of St. Helier's.
  Attorney-General—Thomas Le Breton, Esq.
  Viscount—John Le Couteur, Esq.
  Solicitor-General—John W. Dupré, Esq.

The military defence, laws, and customs are so
very similar in every respect to those of the island
of Guernsey that a repetition would be useless.
The militia of Jersey is a large and efficient force,
in which all persons between the ages of seventeen
and sixty-five are liable to serve. The regiments
are six in number, and muster, with the artillery,
which consists of twenty-four light six-pounders,
about 2500 men. They are in an excellent state of
discipline, and have more than once proved themselves worthy of being entrusted with the defence
of their island home.

———

PLACES OF WORSHIP.

The following dates, recording the consecration, &c.,
will show the antiquity of the respective parish churches
throughout the island, extracted from an ancient manuscript among the records of Coutance, in Normandy.

St. Brelade .... 27th May, A.D. 1111
            Rector—Rev. Ed. Falle, M.A.

St. Martin .... 4th January 1116
            Rector—Rev. George Balleine.

St. Clement .... 29th September 1117
            Rector—Rev. — Marett.

St. Ouen.......... 4th September 1130
        Rector—Rev. Philip Payn.

St. Saviour........ 30th May 1154
        Curate—Rev. J. Wright.

Trinity .... 3rd September 1163
        Rector—Rev. J. T. Ahier.

St. Peter .... 29th June.............. 1167
        Rector—Rev. Philip Filleul, M.A.

St. Lawrence ...... 4th January 1199
        Rector—Rev. T. Orange.

St. John .... 1st August 1224
        Rector—Rev. Philip Dupré.

Grouville.......... 25th August............ 1322
        Rector—Rev. John Mallet.

St. Mary .... 5th October 1320
        Rector—Rev. Philip Guille.

Divine service is performed in the French language in
the above churches, at eleven o'clock, on Sunday mornings, and in the afternoon at half-past two.

Town and Parochial Church, 15th August, 1341.

The Very Rev. Francis Jeune, D.C.L., *Dean and Rector*.

Divine service is performed in French in the morning
on Sundays at eleven o'clock, evening at seven, and in
English at half-past two; also on Thursday evenings, in
French, at seven o'clock, and prayers on Wednesday
mornings at eleven o'clock.

Baptism.—At the Town Church, children born in St.
Helier's parish are baptized on Sunday mornings at nine
o'clock; and, on Wednesdays and Fridays, before or
after service.

Burials.—There are two burial-grounds in the parish
of St. Helier under the jurisdiction of the Dean, but
none belonging to dissenters. Charges for interment

are as follows:—Breaking the ground for a stranger, one pound—Dean's fee: rated inhabitants exempted. Officiating clergyman, five shillings; clerk, two shillings and sixpence; sexton, two shillings and sixpence, and at the Strangers' Ground, and at the New Ground, three shillings and fourpence. Permission to erect a head-stone, five shillings. Tombstones, from three to five pounds —Dean's fee. Churchwardens, Messrs. Edgecumbe and Duhamel.

The Office of the Superintendent Registrar is at Mr. Falle's house, in Church-lane, opposite the church of St. Helier. The office is open from ten to one o'clock daily; Mr. John Sorel is the Superintendent Registrar.

The Office of the Town Registrar of Births, Marriages, and Deaths is at No. 1, Charing-Cross. It is likewise open from ten to one daily. The Registrar is Mr. Henry L. Manuel.

St. Paul's Chapel, New-street.—Officiating Minister, Rev. Mr. Galagher. Service on Sunday, in English, at eleven o'clock in the morning, and seven in the evening, and on Wednesday evening at seven o'clock.

St. James's Chapel, St. James's-street.—Officiating Minister, Rev. S. Langston, A.B. Service on Sunday, in English, at eleven o'clock in the morning, and at half-past six in the evening, and also on Thursday morning at eleven o'clock.

All Saint's Chapel.—Chapel of Ease to the Parochial Church of St. Helier's. Officiating Minister, the Rev. J. Meadows. Service, in English, on Sunday at eleven o'clock in the morning, and half-past two in the afternoon.

Episcopal Chapel of Ease, Gorey.—Officiating Minister, the Rev. C. Robinson. Service, in English, at eleven o'clock in the morning, and half-past two in the afternoon.

Y 3

Dissenting Places.

Calvinist Chapel, Upper Halkett-Place.—Service in the French language, by the Rev. F. Perrott, at eleven o'clock in the morning, and half-past six in the evening.

Congregational Church, Zion-place — Service, in English, at eleven o'clock in the morning, and half-past six in the evening. Officiating Minister, Rev. Mr. Unwin.

Salem Chapel, Ann-street. — Officiating Minister, Rev. S. Carré, in the French language.

Wesleyan Chapel, Peter-street. — In English at eleven o'clock in the morning, and six in the evening. Officiating Ministers, Rev. S. Hope and Rev. J. Sanders.

Methodist Chapel, Don-street.—In the French language at half-past ten in the morning, and half-past six in the evening.

Roman Catholic Chapels.—The Roman Catholics have two chapels in St. Helier's: one in Vauxhall in English,—officiating minister, Rev. Mr. Cunningham,—service at half-past eight and eleven o'clock in the morning; the other, in New-street, in the French language.

PUBLIC INSTITUTIONS.

The Court House, Royal-square.—In this building is held the assembly of the States, together with the Courts of Civil and Criminal Jurisdiction.

The Royal-square was formerly the Market-place, and here Major Pierson lost his life in defence of the island on the 6th January, 1781.

The Market.—Constable, Mr. Chas. Huet; Market days—Wednesdays and Saturdays.

Jersey Signals.—Superintendent, Lieut. Sainthill, R.N.

New Theatre Royal.—Crescent.

Public Library, Library-place.—Mr. Jas. Quesnel, librarian. This building was erected by the Rev. Ph. Falle, a native of Jersey; the venerable historian of the island. He was a Canon of Durham, and Chaplain to King William the Third. The founder enriched the library with an extensive and valuable collection of books in different languages, and left the munificent gift to the island. At a subsequent period, the Rev. Dr. Dumaresq left his voluminous classical library to the collection, and in 1832 the record commission presented it with the Records of England, in seventy volumes folio, since which period the States have, with praiseworthy liberality, voted a grant for its increase, by which many valuable works of modern literature have been added.

Military Arsenal.—This spacious building was erected in 1835. In the lower room is kept the town field battery of six pieces of ordnance, with the harness and all the other material belonging to the artillery. The harness-room is fitted up in the most approved manner, and every article is kept in the highest state of order. The second floor of this building is appropriated for the drill of the militia in the winter months, and is also used for parochial and other public meetings. Being elegantly fitted up and ornamented, it is also used as a public assembly-room. Over the drill-room is a capacious store and armoury, with arm-racks, and every convenience for keeping the arms, accoutrements, and clothing of 1,000 men in the best possible order. In front of the arsenal there is an enclosed parade sufficient for the exercise of a whole regiment.

General Hospital, Gloucester-street. — Governor—

Mr. Sullivan. Governess—Mrs. Sullivan. Physician—
G. M. Jones, Esq. Treasurer—Mr. John Sorel.

*Public Prison and House of Correction, Gloucester-
street.*—Mr. John Kandich, Governor. This establishment is governed by a prison board, consisting of six
members, three chosen by the States, one of whom must
be the Bailli, and three who are members ex officio, viz.,
the Lieutenant-Governor, Viscount, and one of the
Queen's Receivers.

Post Office, Church-lane.—A. Woodgate, Esq., postmaster.—The mails arrive from England by her Majesty's steam-packets, on Sundays and Thursdays. The
mails are made up for England every Monday and Friday
evening. The office closes at nine (mail nights excepted),
then at eleven. Letters put in after nine o'clock, are
subject to the payment of one penny. Letters are also
received at this office, to be sent by private steamers,
viâ Southampton. Post-office orders may be obtained
there also.

Jersey Auxiliary British and Foreign Bible Society.
—Patron, the Lord Bishop of Winchester. President—
Sir John De Veulle. Vice Presidents—Col. Le Cou-
teur and Isaac Gossett, Esq. Treasurer—F. Bertram,
Esq. Secretaries—Messrs. W. Janvrin, G. E. Evans,
and Thomas De Gruchy. Collector—Samuel Cowdy.

Ladies' Branch.—Patron—Lord Bexley. Patroness
—Mrs. General Le Couteur. President—Mrs. Lang-
ston. Vice Presidents—Mrs. A. Pipon and Mrs. Capt.
White. Treasurers—Mrs. D. Janvrin and Mrs. Bluck.

Benefit Society for the Merchant Seamen of Jersey.
—President—Ph. De Quetteville, Esq. Vice President
—Ph. W. Nicolle, Esq. Receiver's Office, No. 9,
New-street.

The Jersey Dorcas Society for Relieving Poor Mar-

ried Women at their Habitations.—Instituted in 1818. Treasurer — Mrs. Brohier. Secretary — Miss M. A. Lempriere.

Benevolent Society.—Patron, Sir John De Veulle, bailli.

Mechanics' Institute and Commercial Association, Beresford-street.

Seamen's Friend Society and Bethel Union.

Jersey Church Missionary Association.—Established in 1822.

The Jersey Religious Tract Society, Museum-street. —Established in 1831. Depository open every Tuesday from one to three. Treasurer—Mr. W. Janvrin. Secretary—Mr. Low.

St. James's School, Clare-street. — Established in 1832. Patron—Rev. S. Langston. Conducted on the British and Foreign School System. Mr. Sims, schoolmaster. Also, a Girl's School, in Providence-street, held at Temperance Hall. Patroness—Miss Moulson. Governess—Miss Wards. On the same system.

Jersey Auxiliary Naval and Military Bible Society. —President—Major-General Sir Edward Gibbs. Depository at the Savings' Bank.

Gorey Daily and Sunday National School.—Instituted August, 1835. Patronesses — Mrs. General Campbell, Mrs. Lemprière (Rozel), and Miss Turner. President — Rev. George Balleine. Vice-President — Rev. Charles Robinson. Treasurer and Secretary— Rev. S. Wright.

Agricultural and Horticultural Society.—Patroness —Her Most Excellent Majesty Queen Victoria. Vice-Patrons — The Governor, Lieutenant-Governor, and Bailli. President — James Hammond, Esq. Vice-Presidents —The Very Rev. the Dean, Thos. Ingle,

Esq., John Durell, Esq., T. R. Lemprière, Esq., C. W. Robin, Esq., James Hodges, Esq. Treasurer—J. J. Le Touzel, Esq. Secretaries—Col. Le Couteur for the agricultural department, and Matthew Noel, Esq., for the horticultural department. Clerk—E. G. Marett, Esq. Board of Management to meet the first Saturday in November, January, March, May, July, and September, at eleven o'clock. Board Room at Mr. Saunder's, seedsman, Upper Halkett-place.

The Jersey Union Infant School, Clare-street, Aquilla-road.—Established August 12, 1833.

The Jersey Athenæum.—President—His Excellency Sir Ed. Gibbs, K.C.B. Vice-Presidents—Sir John De Veulle, W. Walker, Esq., Col. Le Couteur and James Hammond, Esq.

St. Helier's Parochial Sunday School.—Patron—The Right Rev. the Lord Bishop of Winchester.

Jersey District Committee of the Society for Promoting Christian Knowledge.— Patron — The Right Rev. the Lord Bishop of Winchester.

Jersey National School, Upper Don-street.—Patron His Excellency Major General Sir Edward Gibbs, K.C.B. President—The Right Rev. the Lord Bishop of Winchester. Acting President—the Very Rev. the Dean of Jersey. Treasurer—Rev. S. Wright. Secretary—T. Lemprière, Esq.

Jersey Female Penitentiary, Les Pres House.—Patron — Sir John De Veulle. Patronesses—Lady De Veulle, Mrs. General Le Couteur, Mrs. Col. Le Couteur, Mrs. P. Nicolle.

Chamber of Commerce, 1838.—President—Philip De Quetteville, Esq. Vice President—Ph. Winter Nicolle, Esq. Committee—Messrs. Daniel Janvrin, John Durell, Nicholas Le Quesne (son of John), Francis De Ste.

Croix, and Charles Le Quesne. Auditors—Messrs. C. De La Garde, and J. Godfray. Secretary—Mr. John Roissier.

The Jersey Auxiliary to the London Society for Promoting Christianity among the Jews.—Treasurer—Miss Touzel. Secretary—Rev. E. Falle.

The Jersey Ladies' Association to the Irish Society of London.—For promoting the education and religious instruction of the native Irish, through the medium of their own language. Established in 1834. Treasurer—Miss Touzel, d'Hautrée. Secretary—Mr. Lowe.

———

SCHOOLS.

There are upwards of fifty academies and schools, of which I mention a few who receive both boarders and day scholars,

The Rev. Gideon de Joux (Classical and Mathematical), Adelaide House.

The Rev. C. Le Hardy (Classical and Mathematical), St. Manelier, St. Saviour's.

The Rev. C. Robinson (Classical and Mathematical), Union Road.

The Rev. J. C. F. Vincent (Classical and Mathematical), St. Anastasius, St. Peter's.

Mr. Horlock, La Motte House.

E. Neel, Zion House, Longueville.

Mr. Le Feuvre, St. Clement's.

Th. La Cloche, 10, Beresford-street.

R. Spuring, Trinity Road.

E. Wilton, St. Saviour's Road.

M. K. Deuziloe, Albion House, New-street.

Madlle. Malfilâtre, 4, Hemiery-place.

Mrs. Carmichael, York House, Windsor Road.
Mrs. Bennett, La Motte-street.
Mrs. Jarvis, Winchester-place, Trinity.
Mrs. and Miss Howe, Grove Place.
Mrs. Parkes, Coie, St. Saviour's Road.
Misses Malin, Val Plaisant.

NEWSPAPERS, WHERE AND WHEN PUBLISHED.

British Press, Payn's Reading Rooms, 7, Library-place, Tuesdays and Fridays.
Jersey and Guernsey News, Saturdays.
Jersey Times, Bond-street, Tuesdays and Fridays.
Jersey Gazette, 6, Burrard-street, Mondays and Thursdays.
Jersey Chronicle, Royal-square, Thursdays.
La Chronique, Royal-square, Wednesdays and Saturdays.
Le Constitutional, Halkett-place, Saturdays.
L'Impartial, Royal-square, Wednesdays.
Le Jersiais, Royal-square, Saturdays.
Mirroir, Saturdays, Broad-street.

BILLIARD ROOMS.

Divan, Waterloo-street; Gruchy, T., Halkett-place; Gallichan, Royal-square; Sketer, Beresford-street; Slater, W., 60, King-street.

PHYSICIANS.

Consulting Physician.—Matthew Scholefield, M. D., fellow commoner, M. B., Cantab., late President of the Royal Medical Society, Edinburgh, 2, Clarence Terrace.

Banks, S., M. C. S. L., Surgeon, George Town.
Brohier, —, M. D., New-street.
Dickson, E., Grove-place.
Duret, A., 15, Queen-street.
De Caux, —, M. D., La Chasse.
Fixott, Charles, M. R. C. S. L., Beresford-street.
Fixott, John, M. D. C. D. G. M. R. C. S. L., King-
    street.
Grant, St. Aubin's.
Hooper, G., M. D., New-street.
Harding, 23, Beresford-street.
Jolit, Isaac, M. D., 4, Campbell-terrace, Clarendon-
    road
Jones, G., 17 Old-street.
King, R., Beresford-street.
Lowe, —, M. D., St. Aubin's
Le Cocq, M. R. C. S., Hemery-row.
Leigh, A., M. B., 3, Olympic-place.
Lyons, P., Surgeon, R. N., &c., 2 Hyde-place, Claren-
    don-road.
Lequyer, J. B., Surgeon, &c., St. Aubin's.
Mallet, A., Mont à l'Abbé.
Marrett, E., L. R. C. S. L., St. Lawrence.
Nicolle, E., Surgeon, St. Martin's.
Nance, J., 27, Beresford-street.
Preshaw, Union-street.
Quesnel, C., Surgeon, Library-place.
Richards, 1, Aubin-place.
Rowand, M. C., Clarendon Cottage.
Symons, John H., Bath-street.

EXTRACT FROM THE LAW REGULATING BOATMEN'S FARES.

Every boat's crew conveying passengers shall receive from each passenger (his ordinary luggage included):

	s.	d.
From the quay on board a vessel in the harbour	0	3
From the harbour to the small roads	0	6

From do. outside of the Hermitage, or in the great Roads:

	s.	d.
If one passenger only.	2	6
If two passengers only—per passenger . . .	1	6
If more than two—per passenger	1	0

The same sums shall be paid from these several places to the harbour of St. Helier's.

A boatman shall, when required so to do, convey any person or persons wishing to cross from one quay to another, and may only exact one penny from each; should there be but one person, he shall receive twopence.

EXTRACTS FROM THE LAW REGULATING PORTERS' FARES.

The porters may demand the following prices for carrying trunks, and other effects, viz.—9d. from any landing place to the hotels and taverns in the neighbourhood of the Royal-square, and not farther north than the said Royal-square, nor farther east than the south of Halkett-place, nor farther west than the entrance of Pitt-street; one shilling from any landing place to the entrance of Roseville-street, James-street, Hemery-place, Ann-street, to the angle of Charles-street, Minden-

place, Upper New-street, Devonshire-place, Cannon-
street, and Gloucester-street; one shilling and three-
pence from any landing place as far as the extremity of
the parish, on the Grouville-road; as far as the angle
north-east of Simon-place, St. Saviour's-road; as far
as Val Plaisant towards the north, and as far as the entrance of the St. John's-road and Castle Bridge Brewery
towards the west; one shilling and sixpence from any
landing place as far as the stream which separates St.
Helier's from St. Saviour's parish, along the Coie, as
far as the high road of communication from Rouge
Bouillon by Du Val-street, towards the north; and as
far as the junction of the high road leading to Rouge
Bouillon to that of St. John, half way up the hill called
Mont-Martin. It is, however, understood, that the
effects of each passenger thus conveyed at the above rate
shall not weigh more than eighty pounds.

Comparative Value of English and Jersey Currency.

English Currency.	Old Jersey Currency.			Old Jersey Currency.	English Currency.		
£	£	s.	d.	£	£	s.	d
1000	1083	6	8	1000	923	1	6
900	975	0	0	900	830	15	4½
800	866	13	4	800	738	9	2
700	758	6	8	700	646	3	0
600	650	0	0	600	553	16	11½
500	541	13	4	500	461	10	9¾
400	433	6	8	400	369	4	7
300	325	0	0	300	276	18	5
200	216	13	4	200	184	12	3
100	108	6	8	100	92	6	1½
90	97	10	0	90	83	1	6¾
80	86	13	4	80	73	16	11
70	75	16	8	70	64	12	3
60	65	0	0	60	55	7	8
50	54	3	4	50	46	3	0½
40	43	6	8	40	36	18	5½
30	32	10	0	30	27	13	10½
20	21	13	4	20	18	9	2½
10	10	16	8	10	9	4	7½
9	9	15	0	9	8	6	1½
8	8	13	4	8	7	7	8½
7	7	11	8	7	6	9	2½
6	6	10	0	6	5	10	9½
5	5	8	4	5	4	12	3
4	4	6	8	4	3	13	10
3	3	5	0	3	2	15	4½
2	2	3	4	2	1	16	11½
1	1	1	8	1	0	18	5½
s.	£	s.	d.	s.	£	s.	d.
1	0	1	1	1	0	0	11
2	0	2	2	2	0	1	10½
3	0	3	3	3	0	2	9½
4	0	4	4	4	0	3	8½
5	0	5	5	5	0	4	7½
6	0	6	6	6	0	5	6½
7	0	7	7	7	0	6	5½
8	0	8	8	8	0	7	4½
9	0	9	9	9	0	8	3¾
10	0	10	10	10	0	9	2¾
11	0	11	11	11	0	10	2
12	0	13	0	12	0	11	1
13	0	14	1	13	0	12	0
14	0	15	2	14	0	12	11
15	0	16	3	15	0	13	10½
16	0	17	4	16	0	14	9½
17	0	18	5	17	0	15	8½
18	0	19	6	18	0	16	7½
19	1	0	7	19	0	17	6¾

Table of Pounds Sterling in English and Jersey Currency.

Table of Shillings in English and Jersey Currency.

ADVERTISEMENTS.

——◆——

Should the Stranger feel interested in the History of the Channel Islands, the following Works will be found in Redstone's Library, and give every inform- ation that has hitherto been collected relative to their Ancient History, Laws, Agriculture, &c.

CHRONIQUES DES ISLES
DE
JERSEY, GUERNSEY, AUREGNERY, & SARK.
Par George Syrret.

A very interesting book, of which the first part is faithfully copied from an old MS., written in 1331, by a Samuel de Carteret; they are in the old Norman French, but a translation has lately been published in the island.

〰〰〰〰〰〰〰〰

JACOB'S ANNALS OF GUERNSEY,

Is an excellent work, giving a full account of every Public Building and Institution in St. Peter's Port, with a Sketch of the Laws and Customs, and also a concise History of Alderney, and Sark, and Herm.

▲ ▲

DICEY'S HISTORY OF GUERNSEY.

One of the oldest writers, and a good work of reference.

BERRY'S HISTORY OF GUERNSEY.

Not so much esteemed, but containing some information and curious matter.

WARBURTON'S TREATISE on the HISTORY, LAWS, and CUSTOMS of GUERNSEY.

Written by a celebrated Herald and Antiquarian in Charles II.'s time.

QUAYLE'S GENERAL VIEW of the AGRICULTURE of the CHANNEL ISLANDS.

A very good work on the subject.

THE HISTORY OF GUERNSEY.

By JONATHAN DUNCAN, B.A.

Published 1841.

A valuable Work of Reference as to the early History, Antiquities, Laws, and Customs of the Island; contributed to by FERDINAND TUPPER, Esq.

Terms of Reading Room and Circulating Library.

	£	s.	d.
Per Year	3	0	0
Six Months	1	16	0
Three Months	1	1	0
Eight Weeks	0	16	0
Six Weeks	0	12	6
Four Weeks	0	10	0
Three Weeks	0	8	6
Two Weeks	0	7	0
One Week	0	5	0

Terms of the Reading Room.

	£	s.	d.
Per Year	2	0	0
Six Months	1	8	0
Three Months	0	16	6
Six Weeks	0	10	0
Four Weeks	0	8	0
Two Weeks	0	4	6
One Week	0	2	6

B B

Terms of the Circulating Library.

FIRST CLASS.

	£	s.	d.
Per Year	1	12	0
Six Months	1	0	0
Three Months	0	12	0
Six Weeks	0	7	6
Four Weeks	0	5	6
Three Weeks	0	4	6
Two Weeks	0	3	0
One Week	0	1	9

Deposits of 10s. will be required of all who are not Annual Subscribers.

SECOND CLASS.

	£	s.	d.
Per Year	0	10	0
Six Months	0	5	0
Three Months	0	2	6

A Deposit of 10s. will be required of all who are not Annual Subscribers.

W. M'DOWALL, PRINTER, PEMBERTON-ROW, GOUGH-SQUARE.

LaVergne, TN USA
15 March 2010
176053LV00003B/44/A

9 781437 227772